DEDALO AGENCY

BALI
Travel guide

ESSENTIAL TIPS
FOR FIRST-TIMERS,
DIGITAL NOMADS, AND
**UNFORGETTABLE
VACATIONS**

Edited by: Domenico Russo and Francesco Umbria
Design e layout: Giorgia Ragona
Book series: Journey Joy

© 2024 DEDALO SRLS
Bali Travel guide
How to Plan a Trip to Bali
with Best Tips for First-Timers

www.agenziadedalo.it

BALI
Travel guide

Index

INTRODUCTION	9
CHAPTER 1: DENPASAR AND SOUTHERN BALI	15
Bajra Sandhi Monument	16
Denpasar Traditional Market	17
Bali Museum	18
Sanur Beach for Sunrise	19
Kuta, Seminyak, and Canggu Beaches	19
Digital Nomad Hotspots	20
Denpasar by Night	21
Day Trip to Nusa Dua	22
Learning the Balinese Way	23
Final Thoughts	24
CHAPTER 2: UBUD	29
Ubud Royal Palace	30
Art Market and Galleries	31
Monkey Forest	32
Rice Terraces and Organic Farming Tours	33
Yoga and Wellness Retreats	34
Ubud's Best Spots for Digital Nomads	35
Ubud Cuisine	36
Exploring Traditional Dance and Music	37
Eco-Tourism and Conservation Efforts	38
Final Thoughts	39
CHAPTER 3: NORTHERN BALI	45
Lovina Beach	46
Gitgit Waterfall	47
The Ancient Banjar Hot Springs	48
Remote Work in Northern Bali	49
Authentic Balinese Cuisine	50

- Sekumpul Waterfall — 51
- Cultural Immersion — 52
- Snorkeling and Diving in Northern Reefs — 53
- Night Sky Observation — 54
- Final Thoughts — 55

Chapter 4: East Bali — 59
- Besakih Temple — 60
- Mount Agung — 61
- Tirta Gangga Water Palace — 62
- Amed and Tulamben — 63
- Living and Working in East Bali — 64
- Exploring Local Markets and Handicraft Workshops — 65
- Penglipuran and Bangli — 66
- Eco-Tours — 67
- Cultural Festivals and Ceremonies — 68
- Final Thoughts — 69

Chapter 5: The Islands of Nusa Penida and Lembongan — 73
- Kelingking Beach — 74
- Manta Point — 75
- Yellow Bridge and Dream Beach — 76
- Digital Detox and Remote Work Tips — 77
- Island Cuisine and Dining Recommendations — 78
- Adventure Sports — 79
- Seaweed Farming and Local Industry Tours — 80
- Marine and Wildlife Protection — 81
- Learning Local Crafts — 82
- Final Thoughts — 83

Chapter 6: Bali's Cuisine — 89
- Balinese Culinary Staples — 90
- Street Food Tours and Cooking Classes — 91
- Vegetarian and Vegan Options — 92
- Best Spots to Eat and Work — 93
- Traditional Cooking Techniques and Ingredients — 94
- Local Markets — 95
- Seafood Delights — 96
- Coffee Culture — 97
- Culinary Workshops and Chef-led Experiences — 99
- Final Thoughts — 100

Chapter 7: Traveling in Bali as a Digital Nomad — 105
- Choosing the Right Visa for Long Stays — 106
- Finding the Perfect Neighborhood for Long-Term Stays — 107
- Accommodation Options — 108
- Integrating into the Local Community — 109
- Navigating the Local Healthcare System — 110
- Cultural Etiquette and Adaptation — 112
- Managing Health and Wellness — 113
- Maintaining Work-Life Balance in a Tourist Paradise — 114
- Tips for Long-Term Financial Planning Abroad — 115
- Internet Connectivity and Tech Support — 116
- Legal and Financial Considerations for Long-Term Stays — 117
- Coworking Spaces Across Bali — 118
  - Hubud – Ubud — 119
  - Outpost – Ubud and Canggu — 119
  - Dojo Bali – Canggu — 119
  - Tropical Nomad – Canggu — 120
  - Biliq – Seminyak — 120
- Networking and Community Events for Digital Nomads — 120
  - Dojo Bali Events — 121
  - Outpost Events — 121
  - Ubud Writers & Readers Festival — 121
  - Canggu Nomad Meetups — 122
- Best Cafés for Working Remotely — 122
  - Seniman Coffee Studio – Ubud — 122
  - Crate Café – Canggu — 123
  - Coffee Cartel – Seminyak — 123
  - The Loft – Uluwatu — 123
- Final Thoughts — 124

Chapter 8: 10 Must-Have Cultural Experiences in Bali — 129
- 1. Attending a Temple Ceremony — 130
- 2. Participating in a Balinese Dance Workshop — 131
- 3. Visiting Local Artisans: From Batik to Silver Making — 132
- 4. Surfing the Waves of Bali's Famous Beaches — 133
- 5. Exploring Coffee Plantations in Kintamani — 134
- 6. Joining a Local Culinary Class — 135
- 7. Experiencing a Traditional Balinese Healing Session — 136
- 8. Trekking Through the Rice Terraces — 137
- 9. Attending a Full Moon Ceremony in Ubud — 139
- 10. Participating in a Turtle Conservation Program — 140
- Final Thoughts — 141

INDEX — 7

Chapter 9: Recommended Itinerary for a 10-Day Stay — 147

- Planning Your Trip — 148
- Day 1: Arrival in Bali — 149
- Day 2: Exploring Denpasar — 149
- Day 3: Arrival and Initial Exploration in Ubud — 150
- Day 4: Cultural and Natural Highlights — 151
- Day 5: Wellness and Creativity — 152
- Day 6: Journey to Northern Bali and Lovina Beach — 152
- Day 7: Dolphin Watching and Hot Springs — 153
- Day 8: Temples and Palaces of East Bali — 154
- Day 9: Exploring Nusa Penida — 155
- Day 10: Discovering Nusa Lembongan — 156
- Other Itinerary Options — 157
  - Exploring the Gili Islands — 157
  - Diving in Tulamben — 157
  - Cultural Immersion in Tabanan — 157
  - Wellness Retreat in Uluwatu — 158
  - Adventure Activities in Bali — 158
- Final Thoughts — 158

Conclusion — 161

Introduction

Welcome to Bali, the famed Island of the Gods! This enchanting Indonesian paradise offers more than just picturesque beaches and stunning sunsets; it's a vibrant tapestry of culture, nature, adventure, and serenity that draws travelers and digital nomads from across the globe. Whether you're planning your first visit or looking to extend your stay as a remote worker, this guide is crafted to help you navigate Bali's rich landscapes and unique lifestyle with ease and excitement.

Bali is a place where ancient traditions seamlessly blend with modern dynamics, making it an ideal backdrop for both explorative vacations and productive, long-term stays. The island's allure goes beyond its scenic rice terraces and tranquil temples; it's a hub of artistic expression, culinary delights, and thriving social scenes that cater to a diverse array of interests and passions.

In this guide, we'll dive deep into the heart of Bali's most beloved regions, from the bustling streets of Denpasar, with its rich history and vibrant market life, to the serene spiritual center of Ubud, renowned for its arts and crafts, lush landscapes, and as a sanctuary for wellness enthusiasts. We'll explore the Northern regions of Lovina where dolphins play along the sunrise coast and venture to the lesser-traveled East Bali, where the majestic Mount Agung looms over ancient temples and local villages steeped in tradition.

For those drawn to island life, our chapters on the Nusa Islands—Penida and Lembongan—offer insights into spectacular coastal adventures and the quiet charm of seaside living. Here, the pace slows, and the waters invite endless exploration, from snorkeling amidst vibrant coral reefs to kayaking the crystal-clear waters.

Cuisine in Bali is a reflection of the island's cultural mosaic, offering flavors that range from the simplest Nasi Goreng to elaborate ceremonial dishes. We'll guide you through the bustling food markets, introduce you to must-try local dishes, and suggest cooking classes that can offer a deeper understanding and appreciation of Balinese culinary arts.

For digital nomads, Bali is not just a getaway; it's a potential home base. This guide provides comprehensive resources on how to thrive as a long-term visitor, covering practical aspects like visa regulations, coworking spaces, networking opportunities, and tips for integrating into the local community while maintaining a healthy work-life balance.

We haven't forgotten those looking for an immersive cultural experience. Our list of must-have cultural experiences will connect you with the soul of Bali through temple visits, traditional dance performances, artisan workshops, and more, allowing you to engage with the island on a profound level.

Lastly, our recommended itineraries, tailored for stays ranging from a week to ten days, are designed to help you maximize your time on the island. Whether you're looking to soak in as much as possible or find the best spots to relax and rejuvenate, we have options that cater to every type of traveler.

So grab a cup of Bali's famed coffee, settle in, and let us guide you through planning your perfect Balinese adventure. From the moment you land to your last sunset on the island, this guide is here to ensure that your journey is as thrilling, fulfilling, and magical as Bali itself. Let's start this incredible journey together—welcome to Bali!

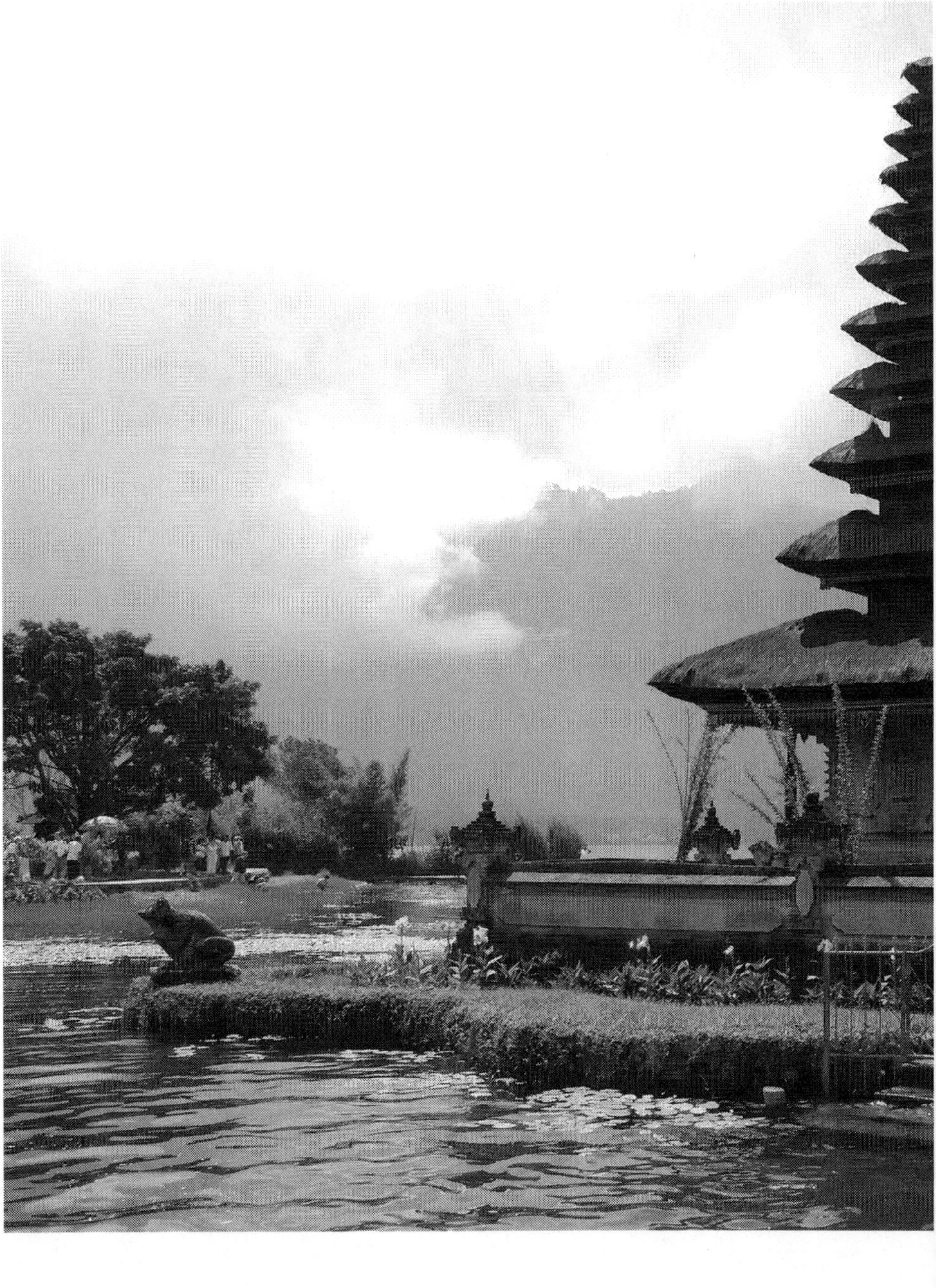

CHAPTER 1: DENPASAR AND SOUTHERN BALI　　　13

CHAPTER 1:
Denpasar and Southern Bali

Welcome to Denpasar and Southern Bali, where the pulse of modernity meets the tranquility of Bali's celebrated beach culture. As Bali's vibrant capital, Denpasar offers a unique blend of traditional Balinese heritage and urban hustle. Moving southward, the vibe shifts to the laid-back rhythms of Bali's famous beaches like Kuta, Seminyak, and Canggu. This chapter aims to guide you through a multitude of experiences from the cultural depths of the city to the relaxing sands of the coast, ensuring a well-rounded introduction to the island's diverse offerings.

In Denpasar, immerse yourself in the city's rich history and lively markets, where the local lifestyle buzzes with authenticity. The journey continues to Southern Bali's idyllic shores, known worldwide for their surf and sunsets. Each location offers distinct experiences, from exploring historical sites and engaging in vibrant shopping adventures in Denpasar to unwinding on the serene beaches and indulging in dynamic nightlife in the south.

For first-time visitors, start your exploration early in the morning to capture the true essence of local life, particularly in Denpasar's bustling markets. Be sure to carry a city map, comfortable walking shoes, and a sense of adventure as you navigate through the city's lively streets. In the southern beach areas, reserve at least a day to relax on the beaches and experience the legendary Balinese sunset. Local transport is readily available, but renting a scooter can give you the freedom to explore at your own pace.

Bajra Sandhi Monument

Standing as a testament to the Balinese struggle for independence, the Bajra Sandhi Monument is not only an iconic landmark but also a deep dive into the island's history. Situated in the heart of Denpasar, this imposing structure is surrounded by the lush gardens of the Renon square, providing a stark contrast to the urban sprawl. The monument's design and the detailed dioramas inside offer a compelling visual narrative of Bali's rich past, making it a cornerstone of cultural exploration in the city.

Visitors can explore the monument's several floors, each dedicated to different epochs of Balinese history, from its ancient kingdoms to its contemporary independence. The architectural grandeur and the poignant exhibits combine to offer a profound insight into the Balinese spirit and resilience. The monument also serves as a vantage point offering panoramic views of Denpasar, making it a favorite among photographers and history enthusiasts alike.

To make the most of your visit, allocate at least two hours to fully appreciate the monument's architectural details and extensive exhibitions. There is a small entrance fee, and guided tours are available to enrich your understanding of each display. Visit early in the day to avoid the heat and the crowds, and wear comfortable shoes as there's quite a bit of walking involved. Don't forget your camera—the view from the top is worth capturing.

Denpasar Traditional Market

Immerse yourself in the vibrant chaos of Denpasar Traditional Market, a bustling hub where the local life of Bali unfolds. Known locally as Pasar Badung, this is the largest market on the island and is teeming with a variety of goods from fresh produce and aromatic spices to colorful textiles and handicrafts. This market is not just a place to shop but a venue to witness the day-to-day activities of the Balinese people, offering a slice of local life and tradition.

The market spans several floors, each dedicated to different types of goods—food and spices on the lower floors, and clothing and crafts on the upper ones. As you navigate through the crowded aisles, the air is filled with the scent of fresh flowers, incense, and local cuisine, providing a sensory feast that is quintessentially Balinese. The market is also a fantastic place to sample local street food, including sweet and savory treats that reflect the island's culinary diversity.

For a successful visit to the Denpasar Traditional Market, arrive early to catch the best activities and avoid the midday heat. Haggling is expected, so don't hesitate to negotiate prices with vendors. Bring cash in small denominations to facilitate easier transactions. Be mindful of your belongings in crowded areas and wear comfortable footwear as you explore the vast market. This visit promises not just a shopping experience but an authentic cultural immersion, giving you a deeper appreciation of Bali's vibrant community life.

Bali Museum

Situated in the heart of Denpasar, the Bali Museum is an essential stop for anyone looking to delve deeper into the island's rich cultural heritage. Housed in several buildings that are themselves architectural gems, the museum showcases a comprehensive collection of artifacts that span from prehistoric times to the contemporary era. These exhibits include traditional Balinese textiles, intricate carvings, religious items, and ceremonial tools, each telling a story of Bali's artistic and spiritual journey through the ages.

As you walk through the various pavilions, you'll notice that each building represents a different architectural style from Bali's various regions, offering a visual feast of traditional designs. The museum's layout is designed to mimic a Balinese village, complete with a central courtyard that hosts occasional cultural performances. This setting not only enhances the authenticity of the experience but also provides a peaceful escape from the city's hustle.

To get the most out of your visit to the Bali Museum, consider hiring a guide available at the entrance who can provide detailed explanations of the exhibits, enriching your understanding of Balinese culture and history. Plan to visit in the morning when the museum is less crowded, allowing you a more leisurely exploration. Check for any special exhibitions or events during your visit, as the museum frequently hosts workshops and cultural performances that are well worth attending.

Sanur Beach for Sunrise

Sanur Beach is renowned for offering one of the most spectacular sunrises in Bali. With its gentle waves and long stretch of golden sand, this beach provides a tranquil alternative to the more bustling southern beaches. The calm waters here are protected by a reef, making it an excellent spot for swimming, especially in the early morning hours as the sun rises over the horizon, casting a warm glow that lights up the beach with soft hues of orange and pink.

The promenade along the beach is lined with a mix of traditional fishing boats and modern cafes, creating a picturesque setting that is ideal for early morning walks. The atmosphere is peaceful, with fewer crowds compared to other popular beaches in Bali. It's a favored spot among locals for morning exercises and ceremonies, adding to its cultural significance and charm.

For an unforgettable sunrise experience at Sanur Beach, plan to arrive just before dawn. Bring a blanket or a beach chair to sit on the sand comfortably as you watch the day begin. Nearby cafes open early, offering a perfect opportunity for a post-sunrise breakfast or a warm cup of Balinese coffee. Make sure to bring your camera to capture the breathtaking views, and if you're up for it, consider renting a bike to explore the lengthy beachfront more extensively after the sun has risen.

Kuta, Seminyak, and Canggu Beaches

Kuta, Seminyak, and Canggu are three of the most iconic beaches in Bali, each known for their distinct vibe and attractions. Kuta Beach is famed for its lively atmosphere and is a hotspot for surfers and party-goers. Moving north, Seminyak offers a more upscale experience with stylish boutiques, luxury resorts, and gourmet restaurants lining the shore. Further north, Canggu is the laid-back cousin, popular among digital nomads and expats, known for its surf breaks, rustic eateries, and vibrant street art.

These beaches offer a comprehensive Bali beach experience from dawn till dusk. Kuta is excellent for those looking to learn surfing with its beginner-friendly waves and abundant surf schools. Seminyak caters to those who prefer lounging in beach clubs with a cocktail in hand, while Canggu is perfect for those seeking a bohemian vibe with its yoga studios and health cafes. To make the most of your visit to these beaches, start your day early in Kuta for a surf lesson when the crowds are thinner and the conditions are ideal. As the day progresses, move to Seminyak to enjoy a luxurious lunch at one of the beachfront restaurants. End your day in Canggu, where you can catch a stunning sunset at one of its many beach bars. Each area offers rental facilities for beach chairs and umbrellas, and remember to stay hydrated and reapply sunscreen throughout the day as you soak up the sun and surf in these dynamic Bali locales.

Digital Nomad Hotspots

Bali has become a haven for digital nomads, thanks to its affordable living, stunning landscapes, and vibrant community of like-minded individuals. Denpasar and Southern Bali, in particular, offer a wealth of options for those looking to work remotely while enjoying the island life. Cafés and coworking spaces are scattered throughout the area, providing reliable internet, comfortable workspaces, and a conducive environment for productivity. Popular spots include Hubud in Ubud, Outpost in

Canggu, and Kembali Innovation Hub in Seminyak, each offering a unique blend of professional facilities and community vibes.

These hotspots are more than just places to work; they are hubs for networking and collaboration. Many coworking spaces host events, workshops, and social gatherings, helping newcomers integrate into the local digital nomad community. Whether you're looking for a quiet corner to focus or a lively atmosphere to spark creativity, there's a spot that caters to your needs. The café culture in Bali is equally impressive, with many establishments offering comfortable seating, excellent coffee, and a welcoming ambiance that makes long working hours feel less tedious.

To make the most of Bali's digital nomad scene, consider purchasing a membership at one of the popular coworking spaces, which often includes access to community events and additional amenities like printing services and meeting rooms. Balance your work with leisure by choosing cafés that offer both strong Wi-Fi and beautiful views, such as those overlooking the rice fields or the ocean. Don't forget to take breaks to explore your surroundings, as the island's natural beauty can be a great source of inspiration and relaxation.

Denpasar by Night

When the sun sets, Denpasar transforms into a vibrant hub of dining and entertainment, showcasing the island's rich culinary traditions and dynamic nightlife. The city offers a plethora of dining options, from traditional warungs serving authentic Balinese dishes to upscale restaurants featuring international cuisine. Popular spots include Warung Wardani for its famous nasi campur and Massimo for delicious Italian fare. Night markets like Pasar Kereneng come alive in the evening, offering a variety of street food that lets you sample a wide range of local flavors.

Entertainment in Denpasar ranges from live music performances in cozy bars to cultural shows featuring traditional Balinese dance and gamelan music. Venues like The Shady Shack in Canggu and Hard Rock Café in Kuta are popular for their lively atmospheres and diverse music scenes. For a more laid-back evening, consider visiting one of the city's many beach clubs, where you can enjoy cocktails and DJ sets with your feet in the sand and the sound of the waves in the background.

To experience Denpasar's nightlife to the fullest, start your evening with a stroll through a night market, sampling various street foods as you go. After dinner, head to a live music venue or a beach club for drinks and entertainment. Always plan your transport in advance, as the city's traffic can be challenging, especially at night. Taxis and ride-hailing services like Gojek and Grab are widely available and convenient for getting around safely.

Day Trip to Nusa Dua

Nusa Dua, located on the southeastern coast of Bali, is renowned for its pristine beaches, luxurious resorts, and world-class facilities. This area offers a perfect day trip destination for those looking to escape the hustle and bustle of Denpasar and indulge in a more tranquil setting. Nusa Dua's coastline is lined with some of Bali's most beautiful beaches, including Geger Beach and Pantai Mengiat, where calm waters and soft sands create an idyllic environment for swimming and sunbathing.

Beyond its beaches, Nusa Dua is home to several cultural and recreational attractions. The Pasifika Museum showcases an impressive collection of art from the Asia-Pacific region, while the Waterblow site offers dramatic ocean views where waves crash against limestone cliffs. For those interested in shopping, the Bali Collection shopping complex features a variety of boutiques, restaurants, and entertainment options. Golf enthusiasts can also enjoy a round at the Bali National Golf Club, known for its scenic course and excellent facilities.

To make the most of your day trip to Nusa Dua, start early to enjoy the morning calm on the beaches. Pack essentials like sunscreen, swimwear, and a change of clothes if you plan to explore other attractions. Renting a scooter or hiring a driver for the day can give you the flexibility to move around at your own pace. Don't miss the opportunity to dine at one of the beachfront restaurants, where you can savor fresh seafood while enjoying panoramic views of the Indian Ocean.

Learning the Balinese Way

Delving into the cultural and historical fabric of Bali is an essential part of truly understanding the island. Bali's rich traditions and historical narratives are preserved through its temples, rituals, and daily practices. In Denpasar, landmarks such as the Pura Jagatnatha temple offer a glimpse into the spiritual life of the Balinese people. This temple, dedicated to the supreme god Sanghyang Widi Wasa, showcases intricate stone carvings and a peaceful atmosphere that invites contemplation and respect.

The city's cultural centers, such as the Taman Budaya Art Center, provide deeper insights into Bali's artistic heritage. Here, you can witness traditional dance performances, music recitals, and art exhibitions that highlight the island's creative spirit. Additionally, visiting local craft markets allows you to observe and purchase handmade goods, such as batik textiles and silver jewelry, directly from the artisans, supporting the preservation of these ancient crafts.

To immerse yourself fully in Balinese culture, consider participating in workshops and classes that teach traditional arts and crafts. These experiences not only enhance your appreciation of the island's heritage but also provide a hands-on understanding of the skills and dedication involved. Respect local customs by dressing modestly, especially when visiting temples, and by learning a few basic phrases in Bahasa Indonesia to engage more meaningfully with the locals. Exploring these cultural and historical sites with a knowledgeable guide can also enrich your experience, offering context and stories that bring the island's history to life.

Final Thoughts

As you prepare to conclude your journey through Denpasar and Southern Bali, keep in mind that the island's true charm lies in its blend of natural beauty, vibrant culture, and warm hospitality. While popular destinations like Kuta and Seminyak offer plenty of attractions, don't miss the chance to explore lesser-known gems such as the traditional villages surrounding Denpasar or the serene beaches of Nusa Dua. Each corner of this region has its own unique story and atmosphere, waiting to be discovered.

When planning your visit, consider the best times to travel to avoid peak tourist seasons and enjoy a more relaxed experience. Balinese festivals and ceremonies, which occur throughout the year, provide unique opportunities to witness local traditions and community spirit in action. Remember to approach your travels with an open heart and a respectful attitude, as these qualities will enrich your interactions and deepen your appreciation of the island's culture.

Lastly, take advantage of the numerous resources available for tourists, including local tourist information centers, which can offer updated advice on events, activities, and safety tips. By embracing the Balinese way of life, even if just for a short time, you'll leave with unforgettable memories and a newfound respect for this remarkable island. Enjoy every moment of your journey in Bali, and let the spirit of pura vida guide you to new adventures and meaningful connections.

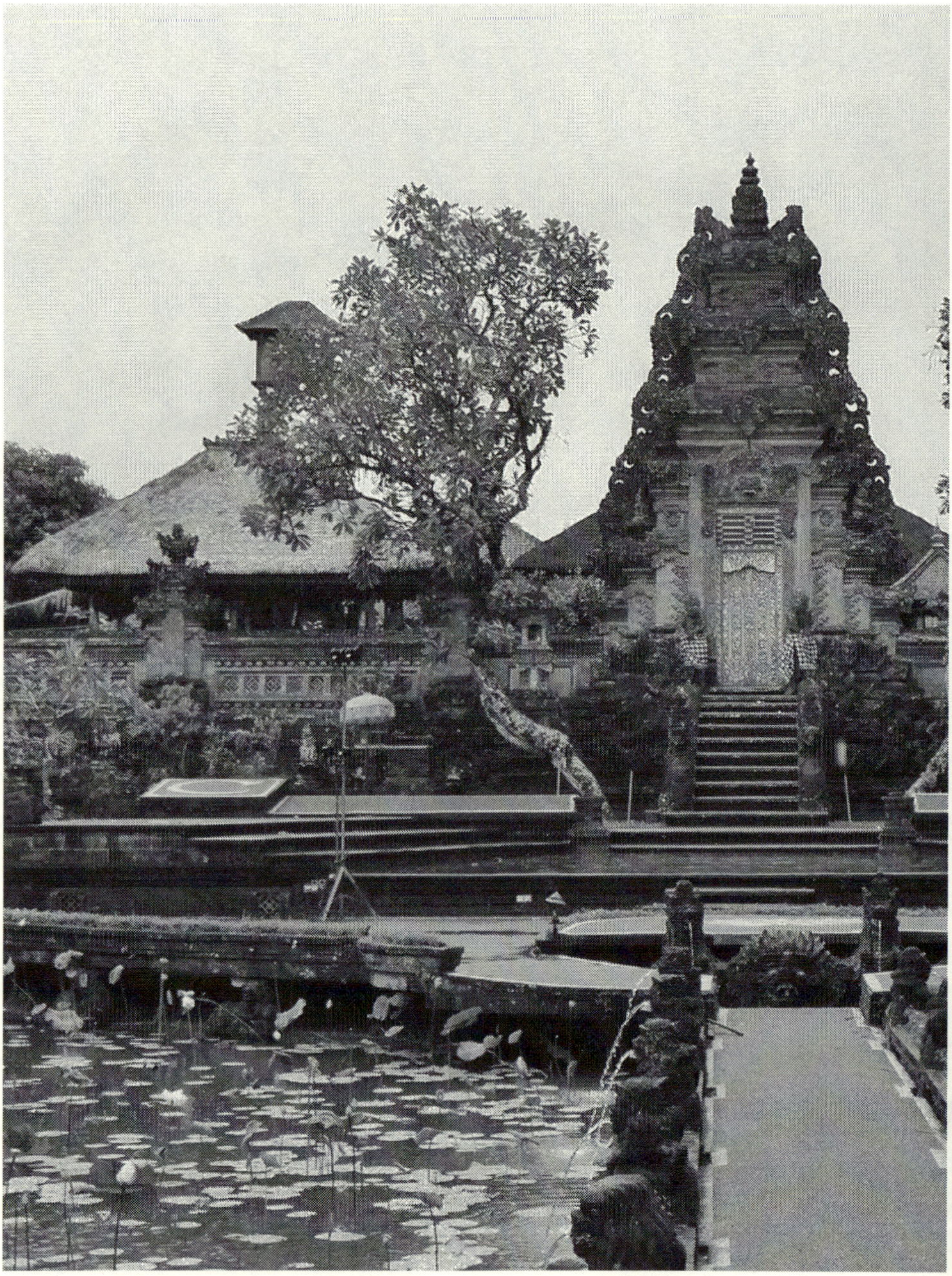

CHAPTER 2: UBUD 27

CHAPTER 2:
Ubud

Nestled in the central highlands of Bali, Ubud is often regarded as the cultural heartbeat of the island. Known for its lush landscapes, vibrant arts scene, and spiritual serenity, Ubud offers a stark contrast to the bustling beaches of southern Bali. This town is a sanctuary for artists, yogis, and travelers seeking a deeper connection to Balinese culture and nature. From its majestic temples and traditional dance performances to the tranquil rice terraces and world-renowned wellness retreats, Ubud captivates visitors with its unique blend of spirituality and creativity.

Ubud's charm lies in its ability to blend tradition with modernity. While it serves as a hub for traditional arts and crafts, it also caters to contemporary needs with its myriad of cafés, coworking spaces, and upscale dining options. The town is surrounded by scenic beauty, including terraced rice paddies, dense jungles, and flowing rivers, making it a perfect destination for eco-tourism and outdoor activities. Whether you are here to explore its artistic heritage, indulge in wellness practices, or simply relax in its serene environment, Ubud promises an enriching experience. To fully appreciate Ubud, allow yourself to slow down and immerse in its rhythms. Early mornings are ideal for exploring the quieter side of the town, while evenings bring cultural performances and bustling night markets. Stay flexible with your itinerary to accommodate the spontaneous discoveries that make Ubud so enchanting. Whether you're visiting for a few days or settling in for a longer stay, Ubud's welcoming atmosphere and rich cultural tapestry will leave a lasting impression.

Ubud Royal Palace

At the heart of Ubud lies the Ubud Royal Palace (Puri Saren Agung), a historical landmark that offers a glimpse into the regal past of the town. Built in the 1800s, the palace serves as the residence of Ubud's royal family and stands as a testament to traditional Balinese architecture. The intricate carvings and ornate gates of the palace compound reflect the island's artistic excellence, while the well-maintained gardens provide a tranquil escape from the town's bustling streets.

Visitors are welcome to explore the palace grounds, which are free to enter and open to the public during daylight hours. The central courtyard is often used for traditional dance performances, particularly the Legong dance, which is a must-see for anyone interested in Balinese culture. These performances, held in the evening, offer a captivating display of intricate movements and vibrant costumes, set against the backdrop of the beautifully illuminated palace.

To make the most of your visit to the Ubud Royal Palace, plan to arrive early in the morning or late in the afternoon to avoid the peak tourist crowds. Check the schedule for cultural performances and arrive early to secure a good seat. Photography is allowed, so bring your camera to capture the stunning architectural details and the lively atmosphere of the performances. Combine your visit with a stroll through the nearby Ubud Art Market to complete your cultural exploration.

Art Market and Galleries

Ubud's Art Market (Pasar Seni Ubud) is a bustling hub of creativity, offering a wide array of handcrafted goods that showcase the island's rich artistic heritage. Located in the heart of town, the market is divided into two main sections: the west side, where you'll find high-quality art pieces and crafts, and the east side, which offers more everyday items and souvenirs. From intricate wood carvings and vibrant paintings to delicate batik fabrics and handmade jewelry, the market is a treasure trove for those looking to bring a piece of Bali home with them.

The art scene in Ubud extends beyond the market, with numerous galleries dotting the town. Renowned galleries such as the Agung Rai Museum of Art (ARMA) and the Neka Art Museum showcase extensive collections of traditional and contemporary Balinese art. These galleries not only exhibit works by local artists but also host regular events and workshops, providing deeper insights into Bali's artistic traditions and modern expressions.

To navigate Ubud's art market and galleries effectively, start your visit early to avoid the midday heat and larger crowds. Bring cash, as many vendors do not accept credit cards, and be prepared to haggle for the best prices, especially in the market. Spend an afternoon visiting the major galleries to gain a broader perspective of Balinese art. Combine your art exploration with a visit to a nearby café or restaurant to rest and reflect on the vibrant culture you've experienced. Engaging with local artists and attending gallery events can further enhance your appreciation of Ubud's artistic spirit.

Monkey Forest

The Sacred Monkey Forest Sanctuary, commonly known as the Monkey Forest, is one of Ubud's most famous attractions. Nestled in the heart of Ubud, this lush forest is home to over 700 long-tailed macaques. The sanctuary not only serves as a popular tourist destination but also plays a significant role in the spiritual and cultural life of the local community. The forest is dotted with ancient temples, including the 14th-century Pura Dalem Agung Padangtegal, which adds a sense of mystique and history to the natural beauty of the area.

Visitors to the Monkey Forest can wander along well-maintained pathways that weave through dense foliage, encountering playful monkeys and discovering the intricacies of the temple architecture. The forest is meticulously maintained, and there are various points of interest, such as the Dragon Bridge and the Holy Spring bathing temple. The interaction between humans and monkeys is closely monitored to ensure the safety and well-being of both.

When visiting the Monkey Forest, it's important to follow the guidelines provided by the sanctuary to ensure a safe and enjoyable experience. Avoid feeding the monkeys or bringing in food and drinks, as this can lead to aggressive behavior. Secure your belongings, as the monkeys are known to be curious and sometimes mischievous. Visiting early in the morning or late in the afternoon can help you avoid the peak tourist hours, and wearing comfortable walking shoes will make exploring the forest more pleasant. This visit offers a unique blend of nature, culture, and wildlife, making it a must-see in Ubud.

Rice Terraces and Organic Farming Tours

The rice terraces of Ubud are iconic landscapes that reflect the island's agricultural heritage and the ingenuity of its people. The most famous of these terraces is Tegallalang, located just a short drive from Ubud's center. These stunning terraces, with their intricate irrigation systems known as subak, are a UNESCO World Heritage Site and offer breathtaking views of lush, green paddies cascading down the slopes. Walking paths allow visitors to explore the terraces up close, providing ample opportunities for photography and quiet reflection.

In addition to the scenic beauty of the rice terraces, Ubud is also known for its organic farming initiatives. Many local farms offer tours that allow visitors to learn about sustainable agricultural practices and the importance of organic farming in preserving Bali's environment. These tours often include hands-on activities, such as planting rice or harvesting vegetables, and provide insights into the daily lives of local farmers. Visiting these farms supports the local economy and promotes eco-friendly tourism.

To fully enjoy the rice terraces and organic farming tours, plan your visit early in the morning when the light is best for photography and the temperatures are cooler. Hiring a local guide can enhance your experience, providing in-depth knowledge about the history and techniques of rice farming. Wear comfortable clothing and sturdy shoes, as the paths can be steep and slippery. Don't forget to bring water and sunscreen, as the Bali sun can be intense. Combining a visit to the rice terraces with a tour of an organic farm offers a comprehensive look at Bali's agricultural traditions and its commitment to sustainability.

Yoga and Wellness Retreats

Ubud is renowned as a global hub for yoga and wellness, attracting practitioners and wellness enthusiasts from around the world. The town offers a plethora of yoga studios, wellness centers, and retreats that cater to all levels of experience. Places like the Yoga Barn and Radiantly Alive are famous for their diverse class offerings, including yoga, meditation, and holistic therapies. These centers provide not only physical and mental rejuvenation but also a sense of community among like-minded individuals.

For those planning an extended stay, Ubud's wellness scene offers a perfect environment for deepening your practice and exploring holistic health. Many retreats offer comprehensive packages that include accommodation, meals, and various wellness activities. These retreats often feature renowned international instructors and offer specialized programs, such as detox retreats, sound healing, and Ayurvedic treatments. The serene environment of Ubud, with its lush surroundings and tranquil atmosphere, provides an ideal setting for these transformative experiences.

When planning a long-term stay focused on yoga and wellness, research the various retreats and studios to find one that aligns with your goals and preferences. Consider booking a retreat that includes accommodation for a hassle-free experience, or choose to stay in one of Ubud's many guesthouses or villas and attend drop-in classes at different studios. Take advantage of Ubud's abundant health food cafes and organic markets to maintain a nutritious diet. Engaging with the local wellness community through workshops and events can further enrich your stay, offering opportunities for personal growth and new friendships.

Ubud's Best Spots for Digital Nomads

Ubud has evolved into a prominent hub for digital nomads, offering a perfect blend of serene natural beauty and robust connectivity. This combination makes it an ideal spot for those looking to work remotely while immersing themselves in Balinese culture. Ubud is home to several coworking spaces that cater specifically to the needs of remote workers, providing high-speed internet, comfortable workspaces, and a sense of community. Popular spots include Hubud, known for its bamboo architecture and vibrant community events, and Outpost, which offers both coworking and coliving facilities.

These coworking spaces are more than just places to work; they are centers for networking and collaboration. Many host regular events such as workshops, networking meetups, and skill-sharing sessions, fostering a strong sense of camaraderie among digital nomads. Additionally, the spaces are designed to inspire productivity and creativity, with stunning views of rice paddies, lush gardens, and traditional Balinese architecture, creating an environment that stimulates both mind and spirit.

For digital nomads planning to stay in Ubud, consider purchasing a membership at a coworking space to take advantage of the full range of amenities and community events. Look for spaces that offer flexible membership plans, including day passes, weekly, and monthly rates. It's also helpful to have a reliable local SIM card for internet access on the go. Combine work with leisure by choosing coworking spaces that are close to popular attractions and health-conscious cafés, ensuring you can balance productivity with the enriching experiences Ubud has to offer.

Ubud Cuisine

Ubud's culinary scene is a delightful mix of traditional Balinese flavors and international cuisine, catering to a wide range of tastes and budgets. Whether you are looking for a simple, budget-friendly meal or a gourmet dining experience, Ubud has something to offer. Local warungs, such as Warung Babi Guling Ibu Oka, serve authentic Balinese dishes like babi guling (suckling pig) and nasi campur (mixed rice) at very affordable prices. These eateries provide a great way to experience local flavors in a casual setting.

For those seeking a more upscale dining experience, Ubud boasts several high-end restaurants that offer innovative takes on traditional dishes as well as international cuisine. Restaurants like Locavore, which is renowned for its farm-to-table approach and creative tasting menus, and Bridges, which offers stunning views of the Wos River, provide memorable dining experiences. Vegetarian and vegan travelers will also find plenty of options, with many restaurants specializing in plant-based cuisine, such as Alchemy and Clear Café.

To enjoy the best of Ubud's food scene, start by exploring the local warungs for an authentic taste of Balinese cuisine without breaking the bank. Make sure to try popular dishes like nasi goreng (fried rice) and sate lilit (minced fish satay). For special occasions, book a table at one of the high-end restaurants well in advance, as they are often fully booked. Additionally, visiting the Ubud Market early in the morning can offer a glimpse into the local food culture, where you can buy fresh produce and snacks. Balancing your dining experiences between local and international flavors will give you a comprehensive taste of Ubud's culinary diversity.

Exploring Traditional Dance and Music

Traditional dance and music are integral parts of Balinese culture, and Ubud is the perfect place to experience these vibrant art forms. The town is renowned for its nightly performances of traditional dances, such as the Legong, Barong, and Kecak dances, each telling stories from Balinese mythology and history. These performances are often held at beautiful venues like the Ubud Palace and Pura Dalem Ubud, where the enchanting music and graceful movements create a mesmerizing atmosphere.

Balinese dance is characterized by intricate hand movements, expressive facial expressions, and elaborate costumes. The Gamelan orchestra, a traditional ensemble featuring a variety of instruments such as metallophones, drums, and gongs, accompanies the dances, adding a rich auditory layer to the visual spectacle. Attending a performance provides a deep insight into the cultural and spiritual life of the Balinese people, as these dances are often performed during temple ceremonies and festivals.

To make the most of your experience, check the schedule of performances at various venues in Ubud and purchase tickets in advance, as these shows can be very popular. Arrive early to get a good seat and take the time to read about the stories and significance of the dances you will be watching. Some venues offer pre-show talks or program booklets that explain the performances in detail. Engaging with these cultural events not only enhances your appreciation of Balinese art but also supports the local performers and keeps these traditions alive for future generations.

Eco-Tourism and Conservation Efforts

Ubud is not only a cultural hub but also a leader in eco-tourism and conservation efforts. The town and its surrounding areas are home to numerous initiatives aimed at preserving Bali's natural beauty and promoting sustainable tourism. These efforts are evident in eco-friendly accommodations, organic farms, and community-led conservation projects. One notable example is the Bali Eco Stay, which offers eco-lodges built with sustainable materials and integrated into the natural environment. Such places emphasize minimal environmental impact while providing unique and immersive experiences for visitors.

In addition to eco-friendly lodges, Ubud boasts several organic farms and permaculture projects that welcome visitors to learn about sustainable agriculture. These farms often offer tours and workshops on organic farming practices, composting, and permaculture design. Visiting these farms not only supports local farmers but also provides valuable insights into how sustainable practices can be implemented globally. The town also hosts various eco-focused events and festivals, such as the Ubud Writers & Readers Festival, which often includes discussions on environmental issues and sustainable living.

To support eco-tourism and conservation efforts during your visit, choose accommodations and tour operators that prioritize sustainability. Look for certifications like Green Globe or other eco-labels that indicate responsible practices. Participate in eco-tours and workshops to learn more about sustainable living and how you can apply these practices in your own life. Additionally, minimize your environmental footprint by reducing waste, conserving water, and respecting local wildlife and habitats. Engaging with these initiatives not only enriches your travel experience but also helps preserve Bali's natural and cultural heritage for future generations.

Final Thoughts

As you plan your journey to Ubud, it's essential to approach your visit with a mindset of respect and curiosity. Ubud offers a unique blend of cultural richness, spiritual serenity, and natural beauty that invites deeper exploration beyond the typical tourist paths. While the well-known attractions like the Ubud Royal Palace and Monkey Forest are must-sees, there are also lesser-known gems waiting to be discovered. Take the time to explore the hidden corners of Ubud, such as the quiet village of Penestanan, known for its artistic community, or the serene Campuhan Ridge Walk, which offers breathtaking views of the surrounding countryside.

For those looking to immerse themselves more deeply in the local culture, consider participating in a traditional Balinese cooking class or joining a local ceremony. These experiences provide valuable insights into the daily life and customs of the Balinese people. Additionally, Ubud's numerous wellness retreats and yoga studios offer opportunities for personal growth and rejuvenation, making it an ideal destination for those seeking balance and tranquility.

Lastly, remember that your journey in Ubud is part of a broader adventure through Bali. Each region of the island has its own unique charm and attractions, from the beaches of the south to the volcanic landscapes of the north. Use Ubud as a base to explore the wider island, taking advantage of the excellent transport links and tour options available. By embracing the local culture, supporting sustainable practices, and seeking out authentic experiences, you will leave Ubud with a deeper appreciation for Bali's extraordinary diversity and beauty. Enjoy every moment of your journey, and may it be as enriching and transformative as the island itself.

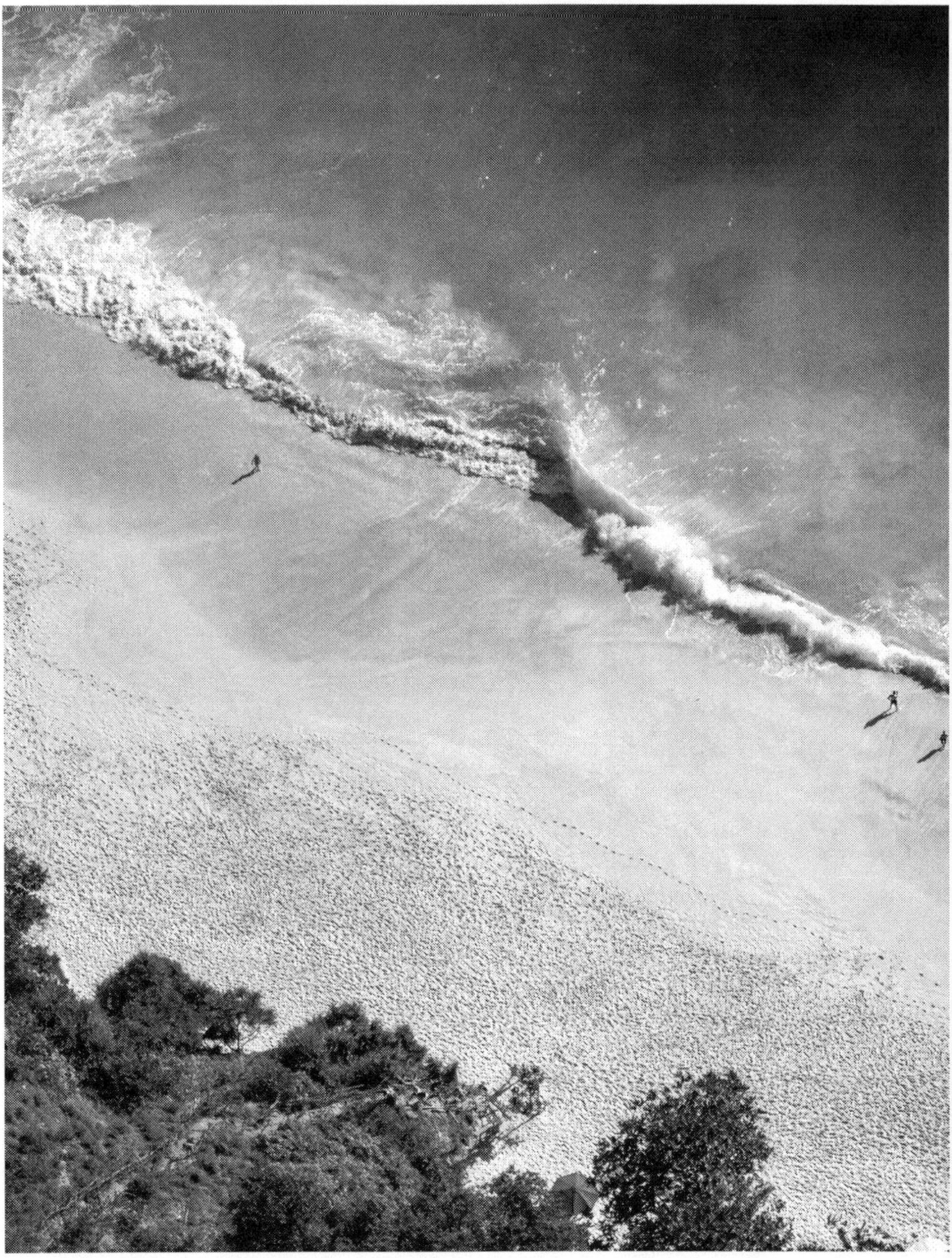

CHAPTER 3: NORTHERN BALI 43

CHAPTER 3:
Northern Bali

Northern Bali offers a serene escape from the bustling tourist hotspots of the south, presenting a landscape rich in natural beauty and cultural heritage. This region is characterized by its tranquil beaches, lush hillsides, and traditional villages, providing a perfect backdrop for a more relaxed and immersive travel experience. Lovina, with its black sand beaches and calm seas, serves as a gateway to the many wonders of northern Bali. From the peaceful retreats of the coast to the majestic waterfalls hidden within the jungle, northern Bali invites you to explore its unspoiled charm and authentic way of life.

The area is less developed compared to the south, allowing visitors to enjoy a slower pace and a more genuine connection with the local culture. Traditional dances, crafts, and ceremonies are still very much a part of everyday life here, offering rich cultural experiences that are often missing in more tourist-heavy areas. The region's natural attractions, such as the serene Gitgit and Sekumpul waterfalls, as well as the therapeutic Banjar Hot Springs, provide opportunities for both adventure and relaxation.

To make the most of your visit to northern Bali, plan to spend several days exploring both its coastal and inland attractions. Early mornings are ideal for dolphin watching in Lovina, while afternoons can be spent hiking to waterfalls or soaking in hot springs.

Staying in locally owned accommodations can enhance your experience, offering insights into Balinese life and supporting the community. With its blend of natural beauty and cultural depth, northern Bali promises a memorable and enriching journey.

Lovina Beach

Lovina Beach, located on Bali's northern coast, is renowned for its tranquil waters, black sand beaches, and delightful dolphin-watching tours. This serene destination is a far cry from the crowded beaches of southern Bali, offering a peaceful retreat ideal for relaxation and contemplation. The calm seas of Lovina are perfect for swimming, snorkeling, and enjoying leisurely boat rides, with the added charm of traditional fishing boats dotting the horizon.

One of the main attractions in Lovina is the early morning dolphin tours. Local fishermen offer these boat trips at dawn, when the waters are calm, and the dolphins are most active. Watching these playful creatures leap and spin in their natural habitat is a magical experience that draws visitors from around the world. The tours are usually conducted in small, traditional boats, allowing for an intimate and close-up view of the dolphins.

To fully enjoy your time in Lovina, book a dolphin-watching tour in advance, as these excursions are popular and can fill up quickly. Arrive early to catch the stunning sunrise over the ocean before setting out on your boat trip. After the tour, spend your day exploring the quiet beaches, enjoying a meal at one of the local seaside restaurants, or simply relaxing by the water. For accommodation, consider staying at one of the beachfront resorts or guesthouses that offer a range of amenities and direct access to the beach.

Gitgit Waterfall

Gitgit Waterfall, one of Bali's most picturesque natural attractions, is located just a short drive from Lovina. Surrounded by lush greenery and tropical plants, this stunning waterfall cascades down from a height of approximately 35 meters, creating a cool and refreshing pool at its base. The walk to the waterfall is an adventure in itself, as the path winds through vibrant forests, past local farms, and over small streams, offering glimpses of Bali's rich biodiversity.

The sound of the waterfall grows louder as you approach, building anticipation for the sight that awaits. Upon arrival, visitors are greeted with the sight of crystal-clear water plunging into the pool below, surrounded by rocks and dense foliage. It's a perfect spot for nature lovers and photographers, providing numerous opportunities to capture the beauty of Bali's natural landscape. The area around the waterfall is also ideal for a refreshing swim or simply relaxing and enjoying the serene atmosphere.

When visiting Gitgit Waterfall, wear comfortable walking shoes as the path can be uneven and slippery, especially after rain. Bring a swimsuit if you plan to take a dip in the pool, and don't forget your camera to capture the stunning scenery. The best time to visit is in the morning when the site is less crowded, allowing you to fully appreciate the tranquility and beauty of the waterfall. Local guides are available at the entrance and can provide valuable insights into the flora and fauna of the area, enriching your visit.

The Ancient Banjar Hot Springs

The Banjar Hot Springs, known locally as Air Panas Banjar, are a hidden gem in northern Bali, offering a rejuvenating experience amid lush tropical surroundings. These ancient thermal springs have been developed into a series of stone pools, fed by naturally warm, mineral-rich water that is believed to have therapeutic properties. The water flows from the mouths of dragon-shaped fountains into the tiered pools, creating a serene and inviting atmosphere for visitors seeking relaxation and healing.

Set amidst beautifully landscaped gardens, the hot springs provide a tranquil retreat where you can soak away your stress and enjoy the soothing benefits of the warm water. The upper pools are smaller and more intimate, while the larger lower pools offer more space for swimming and lounging. The surroundings are lush with tropical plants and flowers, adding to the sense of being in a natural paradise. There are also changing rooms, lockers, and a small café on-site, making it easy to spend a leisurely day at the springs.

To make the most of your visit to Banjar Hot Springs, plan to arrive early in the morning or late in the afternoon to avoid the midday heat and larger crowds. Bring a swimsuit, towel, and change of clothes, as well as a small amount of cash for the entrance fee and any refreshments you may wish to purchase. It's also a good idea to bring water shoes, as the stone floors of the pools can be slippery. After your soak, consider exploring the nearby Brahmavihara-Arama Buddhist monastery for a peaceful and culturally enriching addition to your day.

Remote Work in Northern Bali

Northern Bali, with its tranquil landscapes and slower pace of life, is an ideal location for digital nomads seeking a peaceful environment to work remotely. The region offers a variety of accommodations and coworking spaces that cater to remote workers, providing reliable internet connectivity, comfortable workspaces, and a serene backdrop that inspires productivity and creativity. Whether you prefer working from a cozy café overlooking the rice fields or a dedicated coworking space with modern amenities, northern Bali has options to suit different work styles and preferences.

In Lovina and the surrounding areas, you can find several establishments that welcome digital nomads. Cafés such as Spice Beach Club and Warung Apple offer good Wi-Fi, delicious food, and a relaxed atmosphere where you can work for hours. For those looking for a more structured environment, the Coworking Hub in Lovina provides fast internet, ergonomic seating, and opportunities to network with other remote workers. Additionally, many guesthouses and resorts offer private workspaces and stable internet connections, making it easy to balance work and leisure.

To optimize your remote work experience in northern Bali, choose accommodations that specifically cater to digital nomads, offering amenities such as strong Wi-Fi, comfortable workspaces, and quiet surroundings. Make use of local coworking spaces and cafés to vary your work environment and meet other remote workers. It's also important to maintain a healthy work-life balance by taking breaks to explore the natural beauty of the region, participate in local activities, and enjoy the slower pace of life that northern Bali offers.

Authentic Balinese Cuisine

Northern Bali provides a culinary journey that reflects the island's rich traditions and diverse flavors. The region is known for its authentic Balinese cuisine, often prepared using traditional methods and local ingredients. From savory dishes like ayam betutu (spiced chicken) and babi guling (roast pork) to sweet treats like jaja laklak (Balinese rice cakes), the food in northern Bali offers a delightful array of tastes and textures that showcase the island's culinary heritage.

Local warungs (small family-owned eateries) are the best places to experience authentic Balinese cuisine. In Lovina, Warung Ayu and Warung Bambu Pemaron are popular spots that serve delicious local dishes at affordable prices. These warungs provide a genuine taste of Bali, where you can enjoy meals in a casual and welcoming setting. Additionally, the night markets in northern Bali, such as the Lovina Night Market, offer a variety of street food that allows you to sample multiple dishes in one visit. Here, you can find everything from grilled seafood to traditional sweets, all freshly prepared and bursting with flavor. To fully appreciate the culinary delights of northern Bali, make it a point to dine at local warungs and explore the night markets. Engage with the locals to learn more about the ingredients and cooking techniques used in Balinese cuisine. If you're interested in a deeper culinary experience, consider taking a cooking class, where you can learn to prepare traditional dishes and bring a taste of Bali back home with you. Remember to try a variety of dishes to experience the full spectrum of flavors that northern Bali has to offer.

Sekumpul Waterfall

Sekumpul Waterfall, often referred to as one of Bali's most beautiful natural attractions, is a hidden gem nestled in the lush jungles of northern Bali. Unlike the more accessible waterfalls on the island, Sekumpul requires a bit of effort to reach, but the journey is well worth it. The waterfall comprises seven cascades that tumble down a steep cliff, surrounded by dense tropical foliage, creating a spectacular sight. The crystal-clear water pools below, inviting visitors for a refreshing swim in a serene, natural setting.

The trek to Sekumpul Waterfall involves navigating through local villages, rice terraces, and forest trails, adding to the adventure. The path can be steep and slippery, especially after rain, so it's essential to wear sturdy footwear. Local guides are available to lead the way and share their knowledge about the area's flora and fauna. The trek culminates in a breathtaking view of the waterfalls, where the sound of rushing water and the sight of cascading streams provide a tranquil escape from the everyday hustle.

To fully enjoy your visit to Sekumpul Waterfall, plan your trip early in the day to avoid the heat and larger crowds. Hire a local guide to ensure a safe and informative trek. Bring swimwear, a towel, and a waterproof bag for your belongings, as you'll likely get wet during the hike. Pack a light snack and plenty of water to stay hydrated. This adventure offers a perfect blend of physical activity and natural beauty, making it a must-visit for nature lovers and adventure seekers in northern Bali.

Cultural Immersion

Experiencing village life in northern Bali offers a profound insight into the island's rich cultural heritage and traditions. The region is dotted with traditional villages where life moves at a slower pace, and age-old customs are still practiced daily. Villages like Munduk and Sembiran are known for their scenic beauty and cultural significance. Visitors can witness traditional ceremonies, visit local temples, and observe the daily routines of the villagers, gaining a deeper understanding of Balinese culture.

In these villages, you can participate in various cultural activities, such as traditional dance performances, gamelan music sessions, and craft workshops. These hands-on experiences provide a unique opportunity to engage with the local community and learn about their way of life. Staying in a homestay or a locally-run guesthouse enhances this immersion, offering a more personal and authentic experience. The villagers are often eager to share their knowledge and stories, making your visit both educational and memorable.

To make the most of your cultural immersion in northern Bali, consider booking a stay in a traditional village through a reputable tour operator that supports sustainable tourism. Participate in local activities and be respectful of the customs and traditions. Learning a few basic phrases in Bahasa Indonesia or Balinese can go a long way in building rapport with the locals. Take the time to explore the surrounding areas, including rice terraces and local markets, to fully appreciate the beauty and simplicity of village life. This immersive experience not only enriches your understanding of Balinese culture but also supports the local economy and preserves traditional practices.

Snorkeling and Diving in Northern Reefs

The northern coast of Bali, particularly around the Lovina and Pemuteran areas, offers some of the best snorkeling and diving opportunities on the island. The calm, clear waters are home to vibrant coral reefs teeming with marine life, making it an ideal destination for underwater exploration. Sites like Menjangan Island, part of the West Bali National Park, are renowned for their excellent visibility and rich biodiversity, attracting divers and snorkelers from around the world.

Menjangan Island, in particular, is famous for its stunning coral gardens, steep drop-offs, and abundant marine species, including reef sharks, sea turtles, and colorful tropical fish. Snorkeling and diving tours are available, providing all the necessary equipment and guidance from experienced instructors. These tours often include boat rides to the best spots, ensuring a safe and enjoyable experience. The waters around Pemuteran also feature the innovative Biorock project, where artificial reefs have been created to support coral growth and marine life, offering a unique diving experience.

For an unforgettable snorkeling or diving experience in northern Bali, book a tour with a reputable operator to ensure safety and environmental responsibility. Bring your underwater camera to capture the vibrant marine life and stunning coral formations. If you're new to diving, consider taking an introductory course or a PADI certification program available in the area. Snorkeling can be done directly from the beach in some spots, but boat tours will take you to the prime locations. Respect the marine environment by not touching the coral and avoiding disturbing the wildlife. This adventure provides a breathtaking glimpse into the underwater world and highlights the natural beauty that northern Bali has to offer.

Night Sky Observation

Northern Bali, with its relatively low light pollution and clear skies, offers some of the best stargazing opportunities on the island. Away from the hustle and bustle of the more tourist-heavy areas, the night sky here reveals a stunning array of stars, planets, and constellations. Locations such as Munduk and the area around Lake Buyan are particularly ideal for stargazing, where the elevation and minimal artificial light provide optimal conditions for night sky observation.

Munduk, a quaint village known for its scenic beauty and cooler climate, offers several spots where you can set up for an evening of stargazing. The highlands around Munduk provide a clear view of the night sky, often unobstructed by clouds. Similarly, the shores of Lake Buyan offer a tranquil setting for stargazing, with the calm waters reflecting the celestial display above. Both locations are far enough from the main tourist trails to ensure a peaceful and uninterrupted experience.

For a memorable stargazing experience in northern Bali, plan to visit areas like Munduk or Lake Buyan on a clear night. Bring a blanket, some warm clothing, and perhaps a telescope or binoculars to enhance your viewing experience. Many local accommodations in these areas, such as the Munduk Moding Plantation and Puri Lumbung Cottages, offer stargazing as part of their activities. Check with your accommodation for any scheduled stargazing events or guided night sky tours. Remember to respect the natural environment by minimizing light pollution and noise, ensuring a serene experience for everyone.

Final Thoughts

Exploring northern Bali offers a unique blend of natural beauty, cultural richness, and tranquil retreats that are perfect for those seeking a different side of the island. Beyond the well-trodden paths, this region reveals hidden gems that provide deep insights into Bali's heritage and its stunning landscapes. While Lovina and its dolphin-watching tours are well-known, don't miss the chance to visit lesser-known sites like the serene village of Munduk or the pristine waters of Menjangan Island for exceptional diving experiences.

For digital nomads, northern Bali presents an ideal setting for a productive yet peaceful working environment. Coworking spaces such as the Coworking Hub in Lovina provide excellent facilities and a sense of community, making it easier to balance work and leisure. Additionally, guesthouses and resorts in this region often cater to remote workers, offering reliable Wi-Fi and serene surroundings conducive to focus and creativity. Consider staying at places like Puri Bagus Lovina or The Damai, which offer both comfortable accommodations and inspiring views.

As you plan your visit, embrace the opportunity to engage deeply with the local culture. Participate in village ceremonies, learn traditional crafts, and savor the authentic cuisine that northern Bali offers. Supporting local businesses and sustainable tourism practices not only enriches your experience but also contributes to the preservation of Bali's natural and cultural heritage. Whether you're stargazing in the highlands, diving in coral reefs, or simply relaxing by the beach, northern Bali promises a journey filled with discovery, relaxation, and inspiration. Enjoy every moment and let the serene beauty of this region leave a lasting imprint on your heart.

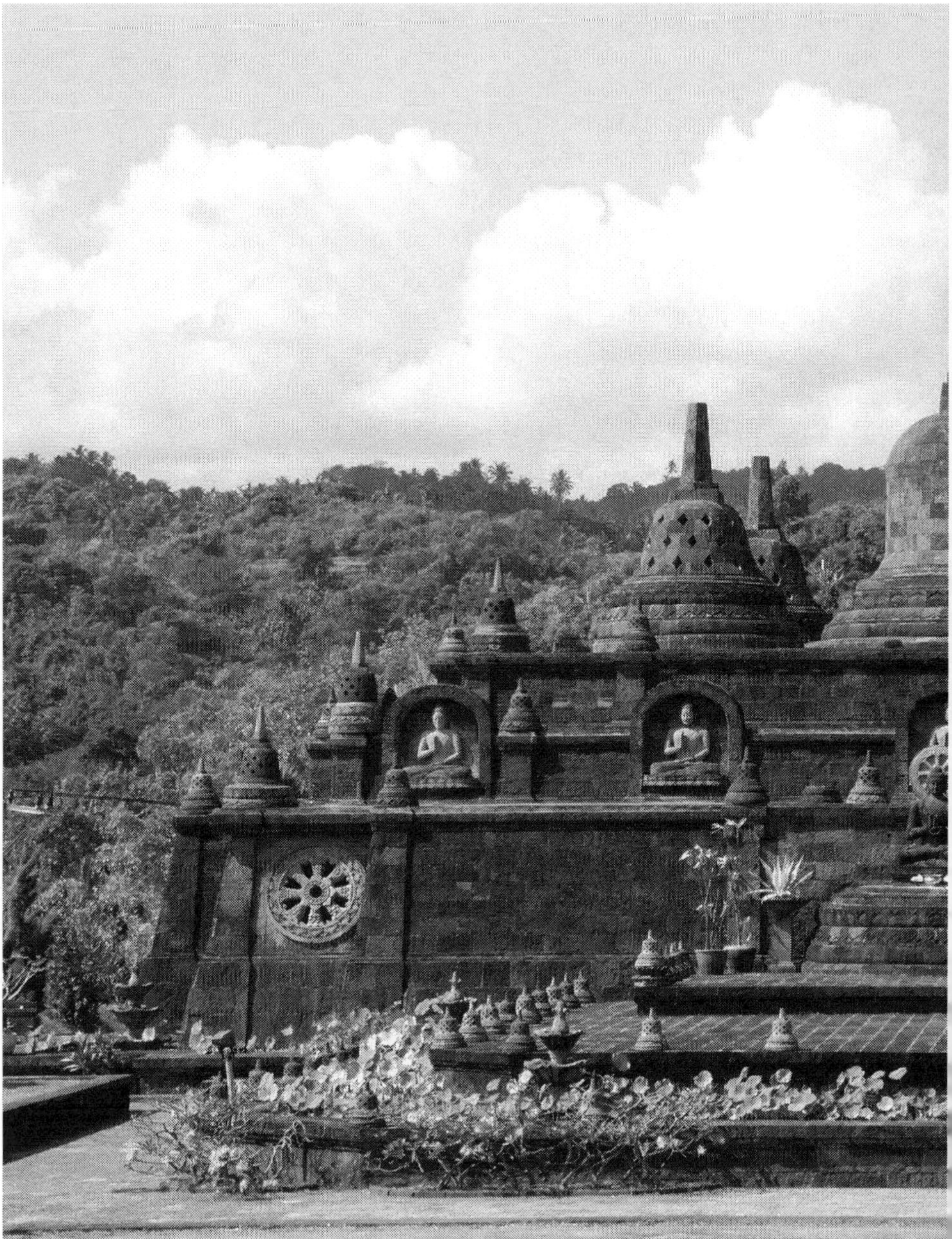

CHAPTER 4: EAST BALI   57

CHAPTER 4:
East Bali

East Bali, with its stunning landscapes and rich cultural heritage, offers a unique and immersive travel experience. This region is characterized by its lush green rice terraces, towering volcanic peaks, and traditional villages that seem untouched by time. Unlike the bustling tourist areas of southern Bali, East Bali provides a tranquil escape where visitors can connect deeply with nature and Balinese culture. From the sacred Besakih Temple, known as the Mother Temple of Bali, to the majestic Mount Agung, East Bali is a treasure trove of natural and spiritual wonders.

The charm of East Bali lies in its diversity and the warmth of its people. Traditional crafts, vibrant markets, and ancient temples offer glimpses into a way of life that has remained largely unchanged for centuries. The coastal areas of Amed and Tulamben are renowned for their pristine beaches and excellent diving opportunities, adding to the region's appeal. Whether you're exploring the intricate water gardens of Tirta Gangga or trekking through the verdant hills, East Bali promises an enriching and unforgettable journey.

To make the most of your visit to East Bali, plan to spend several days exploring both its inland and coastal attractions. Mornings are perfect for visiting temples and hiking, while afternoons can be spent relaxing by the beach or engaging in cultural activities.

Staying in locally-owned accommodations not only supports the community but also offers a more authentic experience. Embrace the slower pace and take the time to interact with the locals, who are often eager to share their stories and traditions with visitors.

Besakih Temple

Besakih Temple, known as Pura Besakih, is the largest and holiest temple complex in Bali. Situated on the slopes of Mount Agung, this majestic temple is often referred to as the Mother Temple of Bali. It comprises over 80 individual temples, each intricately designed and adorned with beautiful stone carvings, making it a significant spiritual and cultural site. The complex is a marvel of traditional Balinese architecture, with its tiered pagodas, shrines, and courtyards that blend seamlessly into the natural landscape.

Visiting Besakih Temple offers a profound insight into Balinese Hinduism and the island's spiritual heritage. The temple is a site of numerous religious ceremonies and rituals, which can be witnessed throughout the year. The panoramic views from the temple complex are breathtaking, with vistas of Mount Agung and the surrounding valleys adding to the serene and mystical atmosphere. The temple's high altitude often means cooler temperatures, providing a refreshing escape from the tropical heat.

To fully appreciate Besakih Temple, hire a local guide who can explain the history and significance of the various temples within the complex. Dress modestly, with shoulders and knees covered, as a sign of respect. Sarongs and sashes are usually available for rent at the entrance if needed. Visit early in the morning or late in the afternoon to avoid the crowds and enjoy the peaceful ambiance. Be prepared for some walking, as the complex is expansive and involves climbing steps to reach different areas. This visit offers a unique opportunity to connect with Bali's spiritual roots and witness its living traditions.

Mount Agung

Mount Agung, the highest point in Bali, is a majestic and sacred volcano that dominates the landscape of East Bali. Standing at over 3,000 meters, Mount Agung is not only a natural wonder but also a significant spiritual site for the Balinese people. It is believed to be the home of the gods and a source of spiritual energy. The mountain's slopes are dotted with temples, including the renowned Besakih Temple, making it a focal point of religious life on the island.

Climbing Mount Agung is a challenging but rewarding adventure that offers breathtaking views and a sense of achievement. There are two main routes to the summit: one from Besakih Temple and another from Pura Pasar Agung. The trek typically begins in the early hours of the morning to ensure climbers reach the summit by sunrise, where they are greeted with panoramic views of Bali and the surrounding islands. The climb is strenuous and requires a good level of fitness, but the experience of watching the sunrise from the summit is unforgettable.

If you're planning to climb Mount Agung, ensure you are well-prepared with proper hiking gear, including sturdy shoes, warm clothing, and plenty of water. Hiring an experienced local guide is essential for safety and navigation, as the terrain can be challenging and the weather unpredictable. Always check the current volcanic activity status before planning your climb, as Mount Agung is an active volcano. For those who prefer a less strenuous experience, exploring the lower slopes and visiting the nearby temples still provides a connection to this powerful and sacred mountain. This adventure offers a unique perspective on Bali's natural beauty and spiritual significance.

Tirta Gangga Water Palace

Tirta Gangga Water Palace, located in the Karangasem regency of East Bali, is a former royal palace renowned for its stunning water features and lush gardens. Built in 1946 by the last king of Karangasem, this tranquil retreat is a masterpiece of Balinese architecture and landscaping, combining traditional Balinese and Chinese design elements. The name Tirta Gangga means "water from the Ganges," reflecting the site's sacred significance and the reverence for water in Balinese culture.

The palace complex is centered around a series of tiered ponds, pools, and fountains, with the iconic eleven-tiered Nawa Sanga fountain being a major highlight. Visitors can wander through the well-maintained gardens, cross stone bridges, and admire the intricate statues and carvings that adorn the grounds. The crystal-clear water of the pools comes from a sacred spring and is believed to have spiritual purification properties. The site also includes a large swimming pool where visitors can take a refreshing dip, surrounded by the serene beauty of the palace gardens.

To fully enjoy your visit to Tirta Gangga, plan to spend a few hours exploring the gardens and relaxing by the pools. Arrive early in the morning or late in the afternoon to avoid the heat and larger crowds. Bring swimwear if you wish to swim in the designated pool area, and a camera to capture the exquisite beauty of the water palace. There is a small entrance fee, and additional charges apply for swimming. Combine your visit with a trip to the nearby village of Ababi, where you can experience more of the local culture and scenic landscapes of East Bali.

Amed and Tulamben

The coastal villages of Amed and Tulamben in East Bali are renowned for their tranquil beaches, vibrant coral reefs, and excellent diving opportunities. Amed is a stretch of fishing villages that offer a laid-back atmosphere, black sand beaches, and stunning views of Mount Agung. It is a popular destination for snorkeling and diving, with many spots accessible directly from the shore. Tulamben, located a short drive from Amed, is famous for the USAT Liberty shipwreck, one of the most popular dive sites in Bali.

The USAT Liberty, a World War II cargo ship, lies just off the coast of Tulamben and is home to a diverse array of marine life, including colorful corals, tropical fish, and occasionally larger species like reef sharks and manta rays. The wreck is accessible to both snorkelers and divers, making it a must-visit for underwater enthusiasts. Amed, on the other hand, offers a range of dive sites such as Jemeluk Bay and the Japanese Shipwreck, each teeming with vibrant marine life and beautiful coral gardens.

For a memorable stay in Amed and Tulamben, book a dive or snorkeling tour with a reputable operator, many of which offer equipment rentals and professional guides. Accommodations range from budget-friendly guesthouses to luxurious beachfront resorts, ensuring options for all travelers. The best time to visit is during the dry season (April to October), when the water visibility is at its best. Don't forget to explore the local villages, where you can experience traditional Balinese culture, visit local markets, and enjoy fresh seafood at beachside warungs.

Living and Working in East Bali

East Bali, with its serene landscapes and slower pace of life, is becoming an increasingly popular destination for digital nomads seeking a peaceful and inspiring environment to live and work. The region offers a variety of accommodations, from rustic guesthouses to modern villas, often with stunning views of rice terraces, mountains, and the ocean. Reliable internet connectivity is available in most areas, making it feasible to work remotely while enjoying the natural beauty and cultural richness of East Bali.

For digital nomads, Ubud remains a popular base with its established coworking spaces and vibrant community, but East Bali also offers excellent options. Places like Amed and Candidasa have begun to attract remote workers looking for a quieter and more laid-back setting. Coworking spaces such as The Bukit in Amed and Co-working Bali in Candidasa provide comfortable workspaces, high-speed internet, and opportunities to connect with other remote professionals. These spaces often host events and workshops, fostering a sense of community and collaboration among digital nomads.

When choosing to live and work in East Bali, consider staying in accommodations that cater to remote workers, such as Bali Marina Villas in Amed or Villa Flow in Seraya, which offer amenities like strong Wi-Fi, workspaces, and serene surroundings. It's essential to maintain a healthy work-life balance by taking breaks to explore the natural and cultural attractions of the region. Engage with the local community by attending traditional ceremonies, visiting local markets, and participating in eco-tourism activities. This approach not only enhances your experience but also supports sustainable tourism and local businesses.

Exploring Local Markets and Handicraft Workshops

East Bali is a treasure trove of traditional crafts and local produce, with vibrant markets and handicraft workshops that provide an authentic glimpse into the region's artisanal heritage. Markets such as the Amlapura Market and the Candidasa Market are bustling hubs where locals gather to buy and sell everything from fresh produce and spices to handmade textiles and ceramics. These markets are excellent places to immerse yourself in the local culture, sample traditional foods, and purchase unique souvenirs directly from the artisans.

In addition to the markets, East Bali is home to numerous handicraft workshops where you can observe skilled craftsmen at work and even try your hand at traditional crafts. Villages like Tenganan and Sidemen are renowned for their weavers, who create beautiful ikat and songket fabrics using age-old techniques passed down through generations. Workshops in these villages often welcome visitors, offering demonstrations and hands-on experiences in weaving, pottery, and wood carving.

To make the most of your exploration of local markets and handicraft workshops, plan to visit in the morning when the markets are at their most lively. Engage with the vendors and artisans to learn more about their crafts and the stories behind their creations. Consider taking a guided tour that includes visits to multiple workshops, providing a comprehensive overview of East Bali's rich artisanal traditions. Supporting these local businesses helps preserve traditional crafts and provides valuable income to the communities.

Penglipuran and Bangli

Penglipuran Village, located in the Bangli regency, is a model of traditional Balinese architecture and community living. Known for its well-preserved culture and environmental consciousness, Penglipuran offers a rare glimpse into Bali's past. The village is famous for its uniform layout, with rows of traditional houses lining a central pathway, each adorned with intricate carvings and well-maintained gardens. The residents of Penglipuran adhere to age-old customs and practices, creating an atmosphere of harmony and cultural integrity.

Nearby, the town of Bangli offers additional cultural and historical attractions. Bangli is home to Pura Kehen, one of the oldest and most beautiful temples in Bali. This terraced temple complex is surrounded by ancient banyan trees and features intricate stone carvings and shrines. Visiting Bangli provides further insights into the region's spiritual and cultural heritage, complementing the experience of Penglipuran.

To fully appreciate Penglipuran and Bangli, spend a day exploring both locations. Begin with a stroll through Penglipuran Village, where you can interact with locals, visit traditional homes, and learn about their customs. Continue to Bangli and explore Pura Kehen, taking the time to admire its architecture and serene setting. Hiring a local guide can enhance your visit by providing historical context and cultural insights. Be respectful of local customs, dress modestly, and always ask for permission before taking photographs of people or their homes.

Eco-Tours

East Bali's diverse landscapes and scenic beauty make it an ideal destination for eco-tours, particularly cycling and trekking. The region's hills and valleys, covered with lush greenery and terraced rice fields, provide a stunning backdrop for outdoor adventures. Cycling tours, such as those offered by companies like Bali Eco Cycling, take you through traditional villages, past ancient temples, and along picturesque rice terraces, offering a unique perspective on rural Balinese life. These tours often include stops at local markets and family compounds, providing opportunities to interact with locals and learn about their daily routines.

Trekking is another popular activity in East Bali, with numerous trails that cater to different fitness levels and interests. Popular trekking routes include hikes up Mount Agung for more adventurous travelers and gentler walks through the Sidemen Valley or the hills around Tirtagangga. These treks allow you to immerse yourself in the natural beauty of the region, with opportunities to see waterfalls, wildlife, and panoramic views of the surrounding landscape.

To make the most of your eco-tour experience in East Bali, choose a reputable tour operator that prioritizes sustainability and community engagement. Wear appropriate clothing and footwear for cycling or trekking, and bring essentials such as water, sunscreen, and a hat. Consider starting your tour early in the morning to avoid the midday heat and to enjoy the tranquil beauty of the morning landscape. Engaging in eco-tours not only provides a memorable adventure but also supports sustainable tourism practices that help preserve the natural and cultural heritage of East Bali.

Cultural Festivals and Ceremonies

East Bali is a region rich in cultural traditions, where festivals and ceremonies play a vital role in the community's spiritual and social life. These events offer a unique opportunity to experience the vibrant culture of Bali firsthand. One of the most significant festivals in East Bali is the Bali Arts Festival, held annually from mid-June to mid-July in Denpasar but celebrated across the island, including in East Bali. This festival showcases traditional dance, music, and crafts, bringing together performers and artisans from all over Bali.

In addition to island-wide festivals, local ceremonies are integral to village life in East Bali. Galungan and Kuningan, for instance, are major Hindu celebrations that occur every 210 days. These festivals mark the victory of dharma (good) over adharma (evil) and involve elaborate offerings, processions, and traditional dance performances. Villages like Tenganan and Sidemen are particularly known for their unique cultural practices and ceremonies, such as the Perang Pandan (Mekare-kare) in Tenganan, a ritualistic fight with thorny pandan leaves that honors the god Indra.

To make the most of your experience at cultural festivals and ceremonies, it's best to plan your visit around the festival dates and be respectful of local customs. Dress modestly, and when attending ceremonies, always ask for permission before taking photographs. Engaging a local guide can provide deeper insights into the significance of the events and help you navigate the complex etiquette associated with Balinese rituals. Participating in these cultural celebrations not only enhances your understanding of Balinese culture but also supports the preservation of these ancient traditions.

Final Thoughts

Visiting East Bali offers a rich tapestry of experiences that blend natural beauty, cultural depth, and a serene way of life. While popular destinations like Besakih Temple and Tirta Gangga Water Palace are must-sees, don't miss out on exploring lesser-known gems like the tranquil village of Sidemen or the vibrant local markets in Amlapura. These places provide a more intimate look at the daily life and traditions of the Balinese people, far from the bustling tourist spots.

For digital nomads, East Bali presents a unique opportunity to balance work and leisure in a peaceful setting. Places like Bali Marina Villas in Amed and Villa Flow in Seraya offer excellent facilities and inspiring environments for remote work. Additionally, coworking spaces like The Bukit in Amed provide a sense of community and professional support, ensuring you can stay productive while enjoying the natural beauty of the region.

As you plan your visit to East Bali, consider incorporating eco-friendly practices into your travel. Choose accommodations that prioritize sustainability, participate in eco-tours, and support local artisans by purchasing handmade crafts. Engaging with the local community, whether through cultural festivals, market visits, or volunteering opportunities, will enrich your experience and contribute positively to the region. Enjoy the slower pace, take time to connect with the people and places you visit, and let the serene landscapes of East Bali inspire and rejuvenate you.

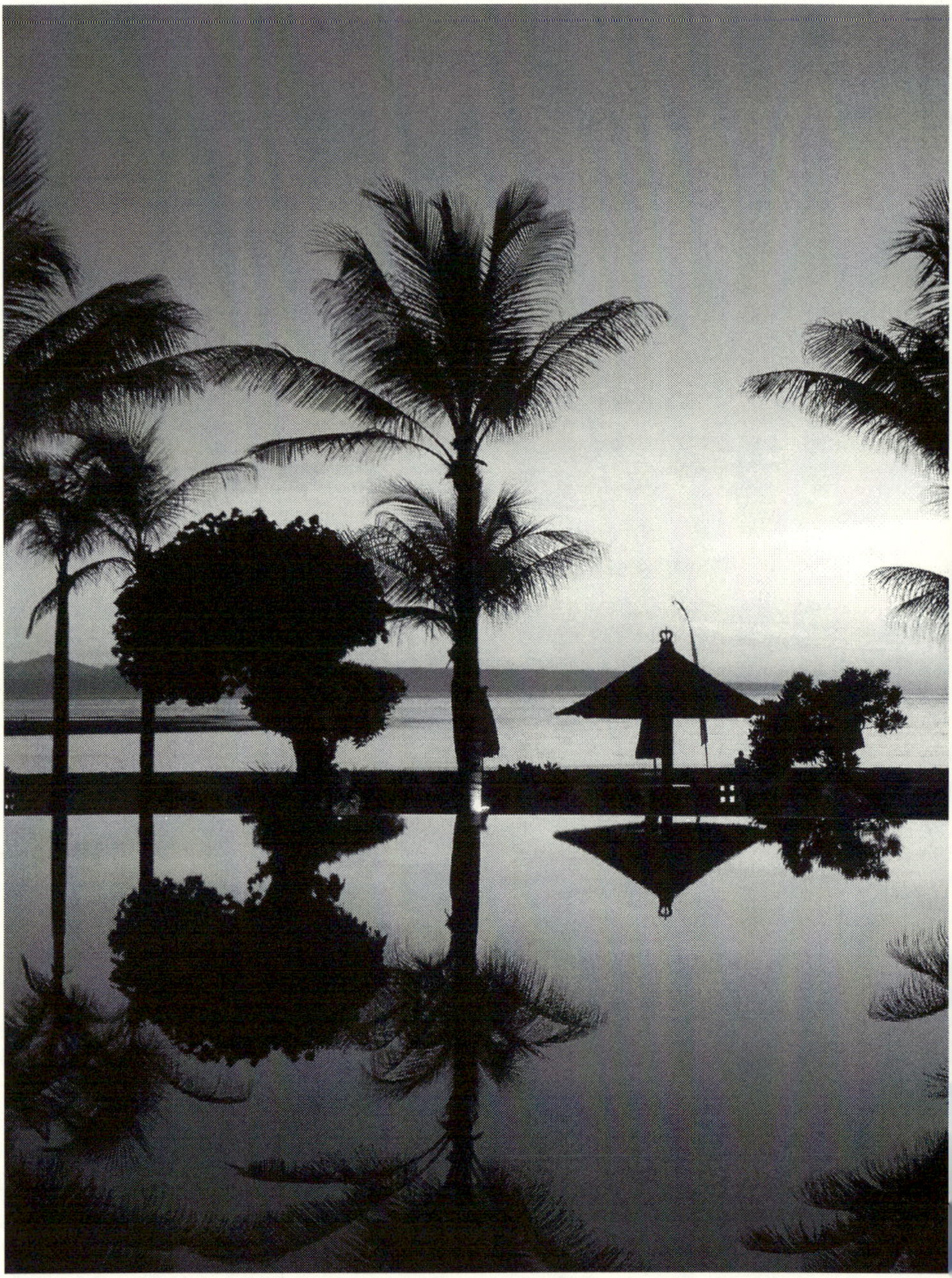

CHAPTER 5: NUSA PENIDA AND LEMBONGAN 71

CHAPTER 5:
The Islands of Nusa Penida and Lembongan

The islands of Nusa Penida and Nusa Lembongan, located just off the southeastern coast of Bali, offer a unique blend of natural beauty, adventure, and tranquility. These islands are less developed than Bali's main tourist areas, providing a more rustic and authentic island experience. Known for their stunning landscapes, crystal-clear waters, and vibrant marine life, Nusa Penida and Nusa Lembongan are perfect for travelers seeking adventure and relaxation in equal measure.

Nusa Penida is the larger of the two islands and is famous for its dramatic cliffs, secluded beaches, and excellent diving and snorkeling spots. Its rugged terrain and less touristy atmosphere make it a favorite among those looking to explore Bali's wilder side. Nusa Lembongan, on the other hand, is smaller and more developed, offering a range of accommodations, dining options, and activities while still maintaining a laid-back island vibe. The two islands are connected by regular boat services, making it easy to explore both during your visit.

To fully enjoy your trip to Nusa Penida and Nusa Lembongan, plan to spend at least a few days on each island. This will give you ample time to explore their unique attractions, relax on their beautiful beaches, and immerse yourself in the local culture. Whether you're diving with manta rays, exploring hidden coves, or simply unwinding in a hammock by the sea, these islands promise a memorable and rejuvenating escape from the hustle and bustle of mainland Bali.

Kelingking Beach

Kelingking Beach, located on the southwestern coast of Nusa Penida, is one of the most iconic and photographed spots in Bali. Often referred to as the "T-Rex Bay" due to the shape of the limestone headland that resembles a dinosaur, Kelingking Beach offers breathtaking views and a sense of untouched natural beauty. The viewpoint at the top provides a stunning panorama of the turquoise waters, dramatic cliffs, and the pristine white-sand beach below.

Reaching the beach itself requires a challenging hike down a steep and narrow path that winds along the cliffside. The descent can be quite strenuous and is not recommended for those who are not physically fit or afraid of heights. However, for those who make the journey, the reward is a secluded and picturesque beach with crystal-clear waters perfect for swimming and relaxing. The beach is often less crowded than the viewpoint, offering a more peaceful and intimate experience.

To make the most of your visit to Kelingking Beach, wear sturdy footwear suitable for hiking and bring plenty of water and sunscreen. Start your hike early in the morning to avoid the midday heat and larger crowds. If you plan to swim, be mindful of the strong currents and waves, as the waters can be quite rough. Take your time to enjoy the views from the top before making the descent, and consider bringing a picnic to enjoy on the beach. The effort to reach Kelingking Beach is well worth it, providing an unforgettable experience of one of Bali's most stunning natural wonders.

Manta Point

Manta Point, located off the coast of Nusa Penida, is one of Bali's premier diving and snorkeling spots, renowned for its regular sightings of majestic manta rays. The site features a cleaning station where mantas come to have parasites removed by smaller fish, offering divers and snorkelers the extraordinary opportunity to observe these gentle giants up close. The clear, warm waters and abundant marine life make Manta Point a must-visit destination for underwater enthusiasts.

Diving at Manta Point is suitable for both beginners and experienced divers, with several dive operators on Nusa Penida offering guided trips and PADI certification courses. Snorkelers can also enjoy the experience, as the manta rays often swim close to the surface. In addition to manta rays, the site is home to a variety of other marine species, including colorful corals, reef fish, and sometimes even turtles and reef sharks. The best time to visit is during the dry season, from April to October, when the sea conditions are calm and visibility is at its best.

To ensure a safe and enjoyable experience at Manta Point, book your dive or snorkeling trip with a reputable operator who prioritizes environmental conservation and safety. Bring a waterproof camera to capture the incredible underwater scenes, and follow your guide's instructions to avoid disturbing the manta rays and other marine life. Wear a wetsuit or rash guard to protect against the sun and any potential jellyfish stings. Respect the marine environment by not touching the coral or feeding the fish, and enjoy the awe-inspiring experience of swimming alongside some of the ocean's most magnificent creatures.

Yellow Bridge and Dream Beach

The Yellow Bridge, also known as the "Bridge of Love," is a charming suspension bridge that connects the islands of Nusa Lembongan and Nusa Ceningan. Painted in a bright yellow hue, the bridge has become a popular spot for photos and a key landmark for travelers exploring these two picturesque islands. The bridge is primarily used by pedestrians and motorbikes, offering a convenient and scenic way to travel between Nusa Lembongan and Nusa Ceningan.

Crossing the Yellow Bridge provides stunning views of the crystal-clear waters below, where you can often see colorful fish and seaweed farms. Once on Nusa Ceningan, visitors can explore the island's hidden gems, including its rugged coastline, small villages, and tranquil beaches. One of the most famous spots on Nusa Ceningan is Blue Lagoon, known for its strikingly blue waters and dramatic cliffs.

Dream Beach, located on the southwestern coast of Nusa Lembongan, is another must-visit destination. This beautiful white-sand beach is framed by rocky cliffs and offers a serene and picturesque setting. The beach is perfect for sunbathing, swimming, and relaxing, with a few beachside cafés and restaurants where you can enjoy a refreshing drink or a meal. The waves at Dream Beach can be quite strong, making it a popular spot for experienced surfers as well.

To make the most of your visit to the Yellow Bridge and Dream Beach, consider renting a scooter to easily explore both islands. Wear comfortable footwear and bring sunscreen, a hat, and plenty of water. Take time to explore the nearby attractions, such as Blue Lagoon on Nusa Ceningan and Devil's Tear on Nusa Lembongan, for more breathtaking views and photo opportunities. Relaxing at Dream Beach is a perfect way to end your day, enjoying the sunset and the peaceful atmosphere.

Digital Detox and Remote Work Tips

The islands of Nusa Penida and Nusa Lembongan offer the perfect environment for both digital detox and remote work, catering to travelers seeking a balance between connectivity and tranquility. For those looking to disconnect and rejuvenate, the islands' natural beauty and slower pace of life provide an ideal setting. Secluded beaches, lush landscapes, and the absence of the usual hustle and bustle make it easy to unwind and enjoy the moment.

For digital nomads, Nusa Lembongan is more developed and offers better connectivity options compared to Nusa Penida. Coworking spaces like Sandy Bay Coworking provide reliable Wi-Fi, comfortable workspaces, and a community of like-minded individuals. Many accommodations also cater to remote workers, offering amenities such as high-speed internet, desks, and quiet environments conducive to productivity. The relaxed island atmosphere allows for a healthy work-life balance, with plenty of opportunities to explore and relax during breaks.

To make the most of your time as a remote worker or while on a digital detox, establish a routine that incorporates both work and leisure. For remote work, set up a dedicated workspace in your accommodation or join a coworking space to stay focused and productive. Take regular breaks to explore the islands, swim, or engage in local activities to prevent burnout. For those on a digital detox, create a plan to limit screen time and prioritize outdoor activities, such as snorkeling, hiking, or simply relaxing by the beach. Engage with the local community and immerse yourself in the island culture to enrich your experience.

Island Cuisine and Dining Recommendations

The culinary scene on Nusa Penida and Nusa Lembongan is as diverse and vibrant as the islands themselves, offering a range of dining options from traditional Balinese dishes to international cuisine. Fresh seafood is a highlight, with many restaurants serving daily catches grilled to perfection or prepared in local styles. Warungs, or small family-owned eateries, provide an authentic taste of Balinese cuisine, including dishes like nasi goreng (fried rice), mie goreng (fried noodles), and sate lilit (minced fish satay).

In Nusa Lembongan, Sandy Bay Beach Club is a popular spot known for its beachfront dining and stunning sunset views. The menu features a mix of international and local dishes, perfect for a leisurely meal by the sea. Another great option is The Deck Café & Bar, located on Jungut Batu Beach, offering delicious food, refreshing cocktails, and panoramic views of the ocean. For a more laid-back experience, try a local warung like Warung Putu, where you can enjoy traditional Balinese dishes in a relaxed setting.

On Nusa Penida, Penida Colada Beach Bar is a favorite among visitors, known for its vibrant atmosphere, great food, and stunning beachfront location. It's an excellent place to unwind with a drink after a day of exploring the island. Amok Sunset, located on the western coast, offers breathtaking sunset views along with a menu that includes both Balinese and Western dishes, making it a perfect spot for dinner.

To fully enjoy the culinary offerings of Nusa Penida and Nusa Lembongan, explore a mix of local warungs and beachside restaurants. Try the fresh seafood and traditional Balinese dishes for an authentic taste of the islands. Remember to check the operating hours and make reservations if necessary, especially for popular spots during peak times. Enjoying the island cuisine while taking in the beautiful surroundings adds an extra layer of delight to your island adventure.

Adventure Sports

Nusa Penida and Nusa Lembongan are ideal destinations for adventure sports enthusiasts, particularly those interested in kayaking and stand-up paddleboarding (SUP). The crystal-clear waters, scenic coastlines, and tranquil bays provide the perfect setting for these activities. Kayaking allows you to explore hidden coves, sea caves, and remote beaches that are often inaccessible by land, offering a unique perspective of the islands' natural beauty.

Stand-up paddleboarding is equally popular, providing a fun and challenging way to navigate the calm waters around the islands. SUP enthusiasts can enjoy the serene environment while getting a full-body workout. The waters around Mushroom Bay and Jungut Batu Beach in Nusa Lembongan are particularly well-suited for paddleboarding, with their gentle waves and picturesque surroundings. Both beginners and experienced paddlers can find suitable conditions and rental equipment to enjoy their time on the water.

To make the most of your kayaking and SUP adventures, rent equipment from reputable operators such as Lembongan Watersport or Newbro Surfing, which offer high-quality gear and guided tours. Early morning or late afternoon are the best times to paddle, as the waters are calmer and the temperatures cooler. Remember to wear a life jacket, apply sunscreen, and bring plenty of water to stay hydrated. Exploring the coastlines by kayak or SUP not only provides an exciting adventure but also offers an intimate connection with the islands' stunning marine landscapes.

Seaweed Farming and Local Industry Tours

Seaweed farming is a significant industry on Nusa Lembongan and Nusa Ceningan, playing a vital role in the local economy and cultural heritage. The sight of seaweed farms, with their neat rows of bamboo stakes and nets, is a common and fascinating feature of the coastal landscape. These farms produce seaweed that is used in various products, including food, cosmetics, and pharmaceuticals. Visiting these farms offers a unique insight into the traditional practices and sustainable livelihoods of the island communities.

Local tours of seaweed farms provide an educational and immersive experience, where you can learn about the entire process of seaweed cultivation, from planting to harvesting and drying. These tours often include opportunities to interact with local farmers, gaining firsthand knowledge of their techniques and challenges. Additionally, some tours combine seaweed farming visits with other local industry tours, such as traditional fishing and salt-making, offering a broader perspective on the islands' economic activities.

To explore the seaweed farms and local industries, book a tour with a knowledgeable guide who can provide detailed explanations and facilitate interactions with the local community. Seaweed tours are available through operators like Lembongan Eco Tour and Bali Eco Tours. Wear comfortable clothing and shoes suitable for walking along the shore. Bringing a hat, sunglasses, and sunscreen is also advisable. Supporting these tours not only enriches your understanding of the islands' industries but also contributes to the local economy, helping to preserve these traditional practices.

Marine and Wildlife Protection

Nusa Penida and Nusa Lembongan are not only known for their natural beauty but also for their significant conservation efforts aimed at protecting marine and wildlife. The rich marine biodiversity around these islands, including coral reefs, manta rays, and sea turtles, has made them focal points for conservation initiatives. The establishment of the Nusa Penida Marine Protected Area (MPA) is a testament to these efforts, covering an area of approximately 20,000 hectares and providing a sanctuary for various marine species.

Several local and international organizations work tirelessly to preserve the marine environment, focusing on coral reef restoration, sustainable fishing practices, and education programs for the local community and tourists. Programs such as the Coral Triangle Initiative and Bali Marine Life Conservation Project are actively involved in these efforts. Additionally, the islands are home to conservation centers like the Friends of the

National Parks Foundation (FNPF) on Nusa Penida, which focuses on reforestation and wildlife protection, particularly for endangered bird species.

To support and engage in conservation efforts during your visit, consider participating in eco-tourism activities such as reef monitoring, beach clean-ups, and educational tours. Dive operators like Blue Corner Dive and World Diving Lembongan offer eco-friendly diving and snorkeling trips, emphasizing marine conservation. Visit conservation centers and participate in volunteer programs to contribute directly to the preservation of the islands' natural habitats. By being mindful of your environmental impact and supporting local conservation initiatives, you help ensure that the pristine beauty and biodiversity of Nusa Penida and Nusa Lembongan are preserved for future generations.

Learning Local Crafts

Engaging in local crafts and cultural exchanges on Nusa Penida and Nusa Lembongan provides a deeper connection to the islands' heritage and traditions. These islands are home to artisans skilled in various crafts such as weaving, pottery, and traditional Balinese painting. Participating in workshops and classes allows visitors to learn these age-old techniques directly from the craftsmen and women who have preserved them through generations.

On Nusa Lembongan, the Lembongan Island Art School offers classes in traditional Balinese arts, including painting and carving. Here, you can spend a few hours or even a full day learning to create intricate designs under the guidance of skilled instructors. In Nusa Penida, the village of Tanglad is renowned for its weaving. Visitors can watch local women weave intricate patterns on traditional looms and purchase beautifully crafted textiles directly from the artisans. These experiences not only support the local economy but also help preserve these important cultural practices.

To make the most of your cultural exchange experience, research and book workshops in advance to ensure availability. Consider joining small group sessions for a more personalized and interactive experience. Engage with the artisans by asking questions and showing genuine interest in their craft. Purchase locally made products as souvenirs, which also supports the artisans financially. These activities offer a meaningful way to connect with the local culture and take home a piece of Bali's artistic heritage.

Final Thoughts

Visiting the islands of Nusa Penida and Nusa Lembongan offers an unparalleled experience of natural beauty, adventure, and cultural richness. While the stunning beaches and diving spots are the main attractions, the islands also provide numerous opportunities for deeper cultural and environmental engagement. From participating in conservation efforts to learning traditional crafts, these islands offer a well-rounded and enriching travel experience.

For digital nomads and long-term travelers, the islands present a unique opportunity to balance work and leisure. Consider staying at accommodations that cater to remote workers, such as Komodo Garden in Nusa Lembongan, which offers reliable Wi-Fi and comfortable workspaces. Engage with the local community by attending village festivals, visiting local markets, and supporting eco-tourism initiatives. This approach not only enhances your travel experience but also contributes positively to the islands' sustainability.

As you plan your trip, remember to respect the natural environment and local customs. Use eco-friendly products, reduce waste, and participate in activities that support conservation. Take time to explore off-the-beaten-path locations, such as the secluded beaches of Crystal Bay on Nusa Penida or the serene Mangrove Forest on Nusa Lembongan. These hidden gems offer tranquility and a deeper connection with nature.

In summary, whether you are seeking adventure, cultural immersion, or a peaceful retreat, Nusa Penida and Nusa Lembongan have something for everyone. Embrace the slower pace, engage with the local culture, and leave with memories and experiences that will last a lifetime. Enjoy your journey through these beautiful islands, and may your travels be as enriching as they are enjoyable.

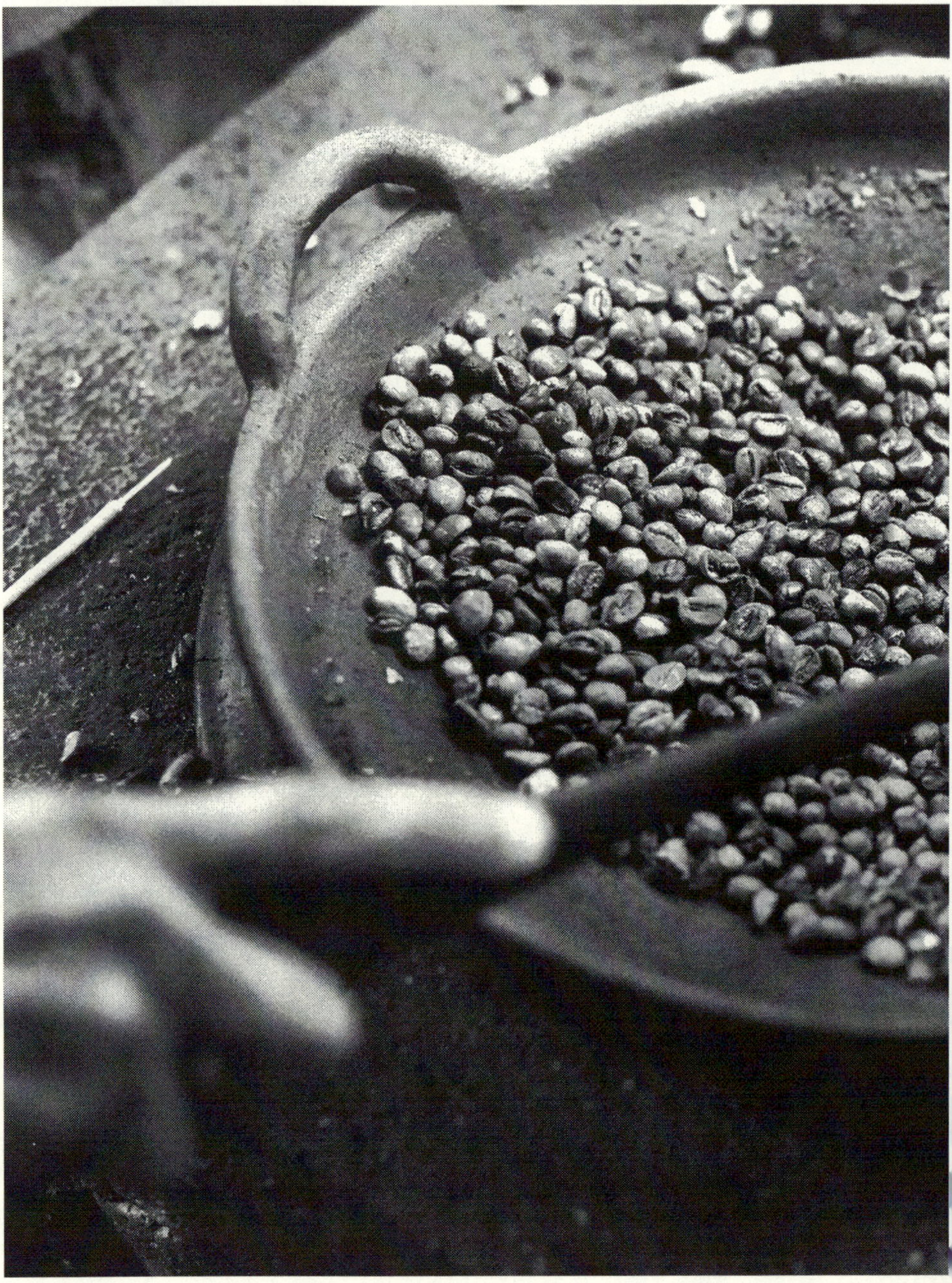

CHAPTER 6: BALI'S CUISINE

CHAPTER 6:
Bali's Cuisine

Bali's cuisine is a vibrant and flavorful tapestry that reflects the island's rich cultural heritage and abundant natural resources. The culinary landscape of Bali is characterized by its use of fresh, locally sourced ingredients, aromatic spices, and traditional cooking techniques. From bustling street markets to high-end restaurants, the food scene in Bali offers a wide array of dishes that cater to every palate. Whether you're indulging in a plate of spicy nasi goreng or savoring a perfectly grilled seafood dish, the island's culinary offerings are sure to delight and inspire.

The essence of Balinese cuisine lies in its bold flavors and aromatic spices. Key ingredients such as lemongrass, turmeric, galangal, and coconut are used generously, creating complex and layered tastes. Meals are often accompanied by sambal, a spicy chili paste that adds a fiery kick to any dish. Rice, the staple of the Balinese diet, is served with almost every meal, alongside an array of vegetables, meats, and seafood. Traditional cooking methods, including grilling, steaming, and slow-cooking in coconut milk, enhance the natural flavors of the ingredients.

To truly appreciate Balinese cuisine, it's essential to explore both its street food culture and its more refined dining experiences. Street food tours offer an authentic taste of local flavors, while cooking classes provide a hands-on opportunity to learn traditional recipes and techniques. Whether you're a foodie, a home cook, or a professional chef, Bali's culinary scene offers endless opportunities for exploration and enjoyment.

Balinese Culinary Staples

Balinese cuisine boasts a number of staple dishes that are both beloved by locals and celebrated by visitors. Among these, nasi goreng and satay stand out as quintessential Balinese comfort foods that showcase the island's unique flavors and culinary traditions. Nasi goreng, or fried rice, is a simple yet delicious dish made with stir-fried rice, vegetables, and a choice of meat or seafood, all seasoned with sweet soy sauce, garlic, shallots, and chili. Often topped with a fried egg and served with prawn crackers, nasi goreng is a versatile dish that can be enjoyed at any time of day.

Satay, another staple of Balinese cuisine, consists of skewered and grilled meat served with a rich and flavorful peanut sauce. The meat, which can be chicken, beef, pork, or fish, is marinated in a blend of spices including turmeric, coriander, and lemongrass, giving it a distinctive taste and aroma. Satay is typically served with rice cakes known as lontong and a side of cucumber salad, making it a satisfying and well-rounded meal. Other popular Balinese staples include babi guling (suckling pig), a ceremonial dish often reserved for special occasions, and lawar, a traditional salad made with vegetables, coconut, and minced meat.

To experience these culinary staples, visit local warungs (family-owned eateries) and traditional markets where you can enjoy freshly prepared dishes at affordable prices. Warung Ibu Oka in Ubud is famous for its babi guling, while Warung Sate Khas Senayan offers a variety of satay options. Don't hesitate to ask for recommendations from locals, as they can guide you to the best places to sample authentic Balinese cuisine. Exploring these culinary staples will give you a deeper appreciation for the flavors and traditions that define Balinese food.

Street Food Tours and Cooking Classes

Exploring Bali's vibrant street food scene is a must for any food enthusiast visiting the island. Street food tours offer an immersive experience, allowing you to sample a wide range of local delicacies while learning about the island's culinary traditions. Guided tours often take you to bustling markets, roadside stalls, and hidden gems where you can taste dishes such as bakso (meatball soup), mie goreng (fried noodles), and pisang goreng (fried bananas). These tours provide a unique opportunity to engage with local vendors, hear their stories, and gain insights into the ingredients and techniques used in Balinese cooking.

In addition to street food tours, cooking classes are a fantastic way to delve deeper into Balinese cuisine. Many cooking schools across the island offer hands-on classes where you can learn to prepare traditional dishes from scratch. These classes often begin with a visit to a local market to source fresh ingredients, followed by a step-by-step cooking session led by experienced chefs. Participants get to enjoy the fruits of their labor, savoring the dishes they've prepared in a communal setting. Popular cooking schools like Paon Bali Cooking Class in Ubud and Bamboo Shoots Cooking School in Sanur offer a variety of courses suitable for all skill levels.

To make the most of your culinary exploration, book a street food tour or cooking class early in your trip. This will not only enhance your understanding of Balinese cuisine but also equip you with the knowledge to appreciate the flavors and techniques used in the dishes you encounter throughout your stay. Bring a notebook to jot down recipes and tips, and be prepared to get hands-on in the kitchen. These experiences will enrich your culinary journey and leave you with lasting memories and skills to recreate Balinese dishes at home.

Vegetarian and Vegan Options

Bali is a haven for vegetarians and vegans, with its abundance of fresh, locally sourced ingredients and a growing number of plant-based dining options. The island's cuisine naturally incorporates a variety of vegetables, grains, and legumes, making it easy to find delicious and nutritious meals that cater to vegetarian and vegan diets. Traditional Balinese dishes like gado-gado (a salad with mixed vegetables, tofu, and peanut sauce), tempeh goreng (fried fermented soybean cake), and sayur lodeh (vegetable stew in coconut milk) are often vegetarian or can be easily adapted to be vegan.

Ubud, in particular, is known for its vibrant vegetarian and vegan food scene. Restaurants like Clear Café, Alchemy, and Sayuri Healing Food offer extensive menus featuring raw, organic, and plant-based dishes. These establishments focus on holistic health and wellness, providing meals that are not only delicious but also nourishing and sustainable. The Seeds of Life, another popular spot in Ubud, specializes in raw vegan cuisine and offers a variety of creative dishes, from smoothie bowls to raw pizzas.

In addition to dedicated vegetarian and vegan restaurants, many traditional warungs are happy to accommodate dietary preferences. Simply ask for your meal to be prepared without meat or animal products. Exploring Bali's vegetarian and vegan offerings is a delightful journey through the island's diverse culinary landscape, proving that plant-based eating can be both satisfying and flavorful.

Best Spots to Eat and Work

For digital nomads and remote workers, finding a conducive environment to work while enjoying great food is essential. Bali offers a plethora of cafés and restaurants that cater to this need, providing not only delicious meals but also reliable Wi-Fi and comfortable workspaces. These spots often combine the island's laid-back atmosphere with modern amenities, making them ideal for balancing productivity with leisure.

In Ubud, Seniman Coffee Studio is a favorite among digital nomads. Known for its artisanal coffee and creative vibe, Seniman offers a relaxed environment with plenty of seating, power outlets, and fast internet. Another popular spot is Lazy Cats Café, which combines a stylish interior with a diverse menu and a welcoming atmosphere for working. For those in Canggu, Dojo Bali is a renowned coworking space that also features an on-site café. With its beachside location, Dojo Bali provides an inspiring setting for work, along with opportunities to network with other remote professionals.

For a mix of good food and a productive workspace, head to The Common in Seminyak. This café and coworking space offers a variety of seating options, from communal tables to cozy nooks, along with a menu that caters to different dietary preferences. Uluwatu's Bukit Café is another excellent choice, offering healthy meals and a relaxed environment perfect for getting some work done.

When choosing a spot to eat and work, look for places that offer comfortable seating, ample power outlets, and a calm atmosphere. Check online reviews and social media for the latest updates on Wi-Fi reliability and crowd levels. Balancing work and dining in Bali allows you to enjoy the island's culinary delights while staying productive and connected.

Traditional Cooking Techniques and Ingredients

Balinese cuisine is deeply rooted in traditional cooking techniques and the use of locally sourced ingredients. The island's culinary traditions have been passed down through generations, with each family and village adding their unique touches to classic recipes. Central to Balinese cooking is the use of a base seasoning paste called "bumbu," made from a blend of spices such as turmeric, ginger, garlic, shallots, and chili. This paste forms the foundation of many dishes, infusing them with rich and complex flavors.

One traditional cooking technique is "panggang," or grilling, which is commonly used for preparing satay and seafood. Meats and fish are marinated in bumbu, then skewered and grilled over coconut husk charcoal, imparting a smoky aroma and tender texture. Another method is "tum," where ingredients are wrapped in banana leaves and steamed or grilled, creating dishes like tum ayam (steamed chicken) that are both flavorful and aromatic.

Rice, the staple of Balinese cuisine, is often cooked using the "kukus" method, where it is steamed in bamboo or clay pots to achieve a perfect, fluffy texture. Coconut milk is frequently used in soups, stews, and desserts, adding a creamy richness to dishes like opor ayam (chicken in coconut milk) and kolak (sweet coconut milk dessert). Ingredients such as fresh herbs, lemongrass, kaffir lime leaves, and galangal are used to enhance the flavors and add a fragrant aroma to the food.

To experience traditional Balinese cooking techniques firsthand, consider joining a cooking class that includes a market visit and a hands-on cooking session. These classes provide a deeper understanding of the ingredients and methods used in Balinese cuisine, allowing you to recreate these delicious dishes at home. Popular cooking schools like Casa Luna Cooking School in Ubud and Bali Asli in Karangasem offer comprehensive classes that highlight the island's culinary heritage. Engaging in these experiences not only enhances your appreciation for Balinese food but also connects you to the cultural traditions that make it so special.

Local Markets

Exploring Bali's local markets is a feast for the senses and a must-do for any food enthusiast. These bustling markets are the heart of Balinese daily life, offering a wide array of fresh produce, spices, traditional snacks, and street food. Visiting these markets provides an authentic glimpse into the island's culinary traditions and the opportunity to taste a variety of local delicacies.

One of the most famous markets is Ubud Market, located in the cultural hub of Ubud. Here, you can find everything from fresh fruits and vegetables to handmade crafts and traditional Balinese snacks like klepon (sweet rice cakes filled with palm sugar). Early morning visits are the best time to experience the market at its liveliest, as locals shop for their daily needs and vendors display their colorful goods.

In Denpasar, Pasar Badung is the largest traditional market in Bali. This multi-level market is a labyrinth of stalls selling an extensive range of products, from exotic fruits and spices to fresh seafood and meats. Pasar Badung is an excellent place to sample traditional Balinese dishes such as nasi campur (mixed rice) and babi guling (suckling pig), which are prepared fresh by market vendors.

For a more coastal experience, head to the Jimbaran Fish Market, where you can buy fresh seafood directly from local fishermen. The market is bustling in the early morning when the boats come in with the day's catch, offering everything from prawns and crabs to a variety of fish. Many vendors will even grill your purchases on-site, allowing you to enjoy a fresh seafood meal right by the beach.

When visiting local markets, it's helpful to go with a guide or a knowledgeable local who can explain the different foods and customs. Wear comfortable shoes and be prepared to haggle for the best prices. Bringing small change is also advisable, as vendors may not have large bills. Exploring Bali's markets is a culinary adventure that offers rich insights into the island's food culture.

Seafood Delights

Bali's coastal regions, particularly Jimbaran Bay and Sanur, are renowned for their fresh and delicious seafood. Jimbaran Bay, located just south of Kuta, is famous for its beachfront seafood restaurants that offer a dining experience like no other. Here, you can enjoy a sumptuous seafood meal with your toes in the sand, watching the sun set over the Indian Ocean. The seafood is grilled over coconut husks, giving it a unique smoky flavor, and is typically served with a variety of sambals (spicy sauces) and side dishes.

The seafood market in Jimbaran Bay is the best place to select your catch of the day. You can choose from a wide selection of fish, prawns, crabs, and lobsters, which are then cooked to your liking by nearby restaurants. Popular dishes include grilled snapper, spicy calamari, and Jimbaran-style clams. Dining at Jimbaran Bay is not just about the food; it's also about the atmosphere and the experience of enjoying a meal by the sea.

Sanur, on the eastern coast of Bali, also offers a fantastic seafood dining experience. Sanur's beachfront restaurants and warungs (small eateries) serve a variety of fresh seafood dishes, from grilled fish to seafood curries. Warung Mak Beng is a well-known spot in Sanur, famous for its fish soup and fried fish served with a spicy sambal. Another notable place is Lilla Pantai, where you can enjoy seafood platters while taking in the serene beach views.

To fully enjoy Bali's seafood offerings, visit these coastal areas in the late afternoon or evening when the seafood is freshest and the ambiance is perfect for a relaxing meal. Don't hesitate to ask the staff for recommendations on the day's best catch. Pair your meal with a local beer or a refreshing coconut drink for a true taste of Bali's seaside culinary delights.

Coffee Culture

Bali's coffee culture is deeply rooted in its rich agricultural traditions and diverse landscape, which provides the perfect conditions for growing high-quality coffee beans. The island is home to numerous coffee plantations, particularly in the Kintamani highlands, where the volcanic soil and cool climate contribute to the unique flavor profile of Balinese coffee. Exploring these coffee plantations offers a fascinating insight into the process of coffee cultivation, from bean to cup.

A visit to a coffee plantation typically includes a guided tour where you can see the coffee plants up close, learn about the harvesting and processing methods, and taste various types of coffee. Many plantations also grow other crops like cocoa, spices, and tropical fruits, making the tours even more diverse and interesting. One of the most popular plantations to visit is Satria Agrowisata, located near Ubud, which offers a comprehensive tour and coffee tasting experience.

In addition to traditional Balinese coffee, the island is known for its production of kopi luwak, or civet coffee, which is made using beans that have been eaten and excreted by the Asian palm civet. This unique and expensive coffee is said to have a smoother and richer taste due to the fermentation process in the civet's digestive system. While it's a controversial product due to ethical concerns, some plantations offer ethically sourced kopi luwak where the civets are kept in humane conditions.

For coffee enthusiasts, Bali also boasts a vibrant café scene, particularly in areas like Ubud, Seminyak, and Canggu. Cafés such as Seniman Coffee Studio in Ubud and Revolver Espresso in Seminyak are well-known for their expertly brewed coffee and cozy atmospheres. These spots are perfect for enjoying a cup of freshly brewed Balinese coffee while relaxing or catching up on work.

To make the most of your coffee journey in Bali, combine plantation visits with café hopping to experience the full spectrum of Bali's coffee culture. Purchase some local beans to take home as a souvenir, and try different brewing methods to find your favorite. Engaging with Bali's coffee culture not only enhances your appreciation for this beloved beverage but also supports local farmers and the island's sustainable agricultural practices.

Culinary Workshops and Chef-led Experiences

Engaging in culinary workshops and chef-led experiences is one of the best ways to immerse yourself in Bali's rich culinary traditions. These interactive classes offer a hands-on approach to learning the secrets of Balinese cuisine, from selecting fresh ingredients to mastering traditional cooking techniques. Many of these workshops begin with a visit to a local market, where you can learn about the various spices, herbs, and produce that are integral to Balinese cooking.

One of the most renowned culinary schools in Bali is the Casa Luna Cooking School in Ubud. Founded by Janet DeNeefe, a celebrated chef and author, Casa Luna offers a range of classes that cover different aspects of Balinese cuisine, including traditional recipes, ceremonial foods, and modern interpretations. The classes are held in a beautiful open-air kitchen and often include a market tour and a communal meal at the end.

Another excellent option is Bali Asli in Karangasem, which provides a unique culinary experience set against the backdrop of Mount Agung. Bali Asli's classes emphasize the use of traditional cooking methods, such as grinding spices with a mortar and pestle and cooking over an open wood fire. The school also offers "A Day in the Life of a Balinese Farmer," an immersive experience that includes farming activities and cooking with locally sourced ingredients.

For a more personalized experience, consider booking a private cooking class with a local chef. Companies like Paon Bali Cooking Class offer private sessions where you can customize the menu and learn at your own pace. These experiences often take place in the chef's home or a traditional Balinese compound, providing an intimate glimpse into local life and customs.

To make the most of your culinary workshop or chef-led experience, book in advance to secure your spot, especially during peak tourist seasons. Wear comfortable clothing and be prepared to get hands-on in the kitchen. Bring a notebook to jot down recipes and tips from the chef, and don't forget your camera to capture the memorable moments. These workshops not only enhance your cooking skills but also deepen your appreciation for Balinese culture and cuisine.

Final Thoughts

Exploring Bali's cuisine is a journey that goes far beyond just tasting delicious food. It's about understanding the island's cultural heritage, engaging with local communities, and appreciating the artistry that goes into every dish. Whether you're enjoying a simple meal at a roadside warung or participating in a chef-led culinary workshop, each experience adds a new layer to your understanding of Bali's rich culinary tapestry.

For digital nomads and remote workers, Bali offers a unique blend of work and leisure opportunities. Many of the island's cafés and coworking spaces, such as Hubud in Ubud and Outpost in Canggu, provide not only excellent facilities but also a community of like-minded individuals. These spaces often host events and workshops that can enrich your stay, from wellness sessions to professional networking opportunities.

When planning your culinary adventures, don't limit yourself to the well-known spots. Explore off-the-beaten-path locations and lesser-known eateries where you can find hidden gems and authentic experiences. Places like Warung Babi Guling Ibu Oka in Ubud or Warung Sate Khas Senayan offer traditional dishes that are beloved by locals and provide a true taste of Bali.

Additionally, consider exploring Bali's neighboring islands, such as Nusa Penida and Nusa Lembongan, for a different culinary perspective. These islands offer fresh seafood and unique local specialties that are worth the trip. Participate in local food festivals and markets, where you can sample a wide variety of dishes and interact with vendors who are passionate about their craft.

In summary, Bali's culinary scene is a vibrant and integral part of the island's cultural identity. Embrace the diversity of flavors, the warmth of the local people, and the opportunities to learn and grow through food. Whether you're a seasoned foodie or a curious traveler, Bali's cuisine promises a journey of discovery and delight that will leave a lasting impression on your palate and your heart. Enjoy every bite and every moment of your culinary adventure in Bali.

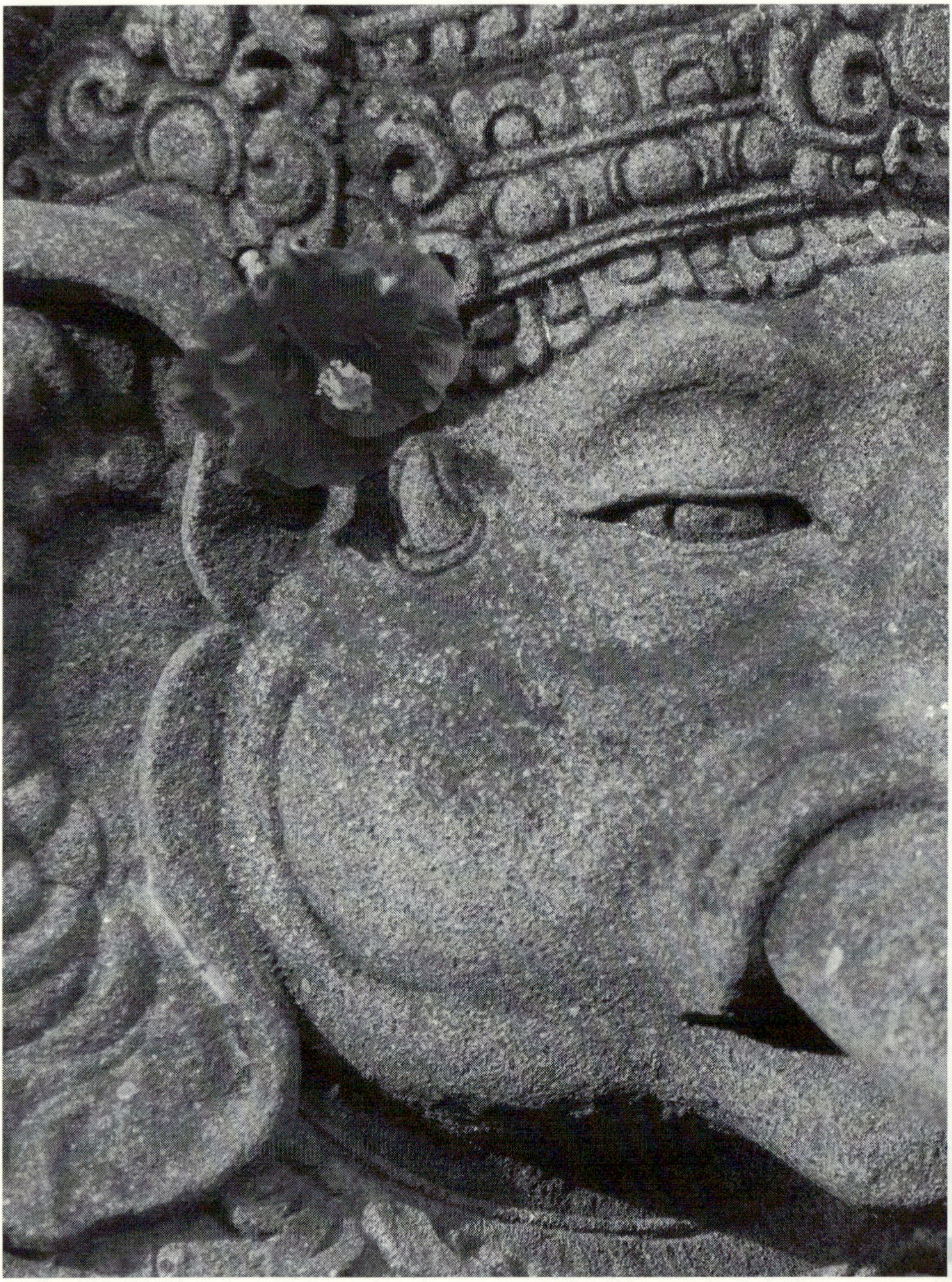

CHAPTER 7: TRAVELING AS A DIGITAL NOMAD   103

CHAPTER 7:
Traveling in Bali as a Digital Nomad

Bali has become a premier destination for digital nomads, offering a perfect blend of stunning natural beauty, vibrant culture, and modern amenities that cater to remote workers. The island's laid-back atmosphere, combined with its burgeoning infrastructure for digital nomads, makes it an ideal place to balance work and leisure. From bustling coworking spaces and trendy cafés to serene beachside retreats, Bali provides a variety of environments that suit different working styles and preferences.

One of the key attractions for digital nomads is Bali's affordable cost of living, which allows for a comfortable lifestyle without breaking the bank. The island offers a wide range of accommodation options, from budget-friendly guesthouses to luxurious villas, and a thriving food scene that caters to all tastes and dietary needs. Additionally, Bali's welcoming community of digital nomads and expats provides ample opportunities for networking, collaboration, and socializing.

To make the most of your time in Bali as a digital nomad, it's important to plan ahead and familiarize yourself with the island's resources and regulations. Understanding visa requirements, finding suitable accommodation, and choosing the right coworking spaces are essential steps to ensure a smooth and productive stay. By preparing adequately, you can fully enjoy the unique lifestyle that Bali offers to remote workers.

Choosing the Right Visa for Long Stays

Navigating the visa requirements for long-term stays in Bali is a crucial step for digital nomads planning to work remotely from the island. Indonesia offers several visa options that can cater to different needs and durations of stay. The most common visas for digital nomads include the Tourist Visa, the Social-Cultural Visa (B211A), and the Business Visa.

The Tourist Visa is typically valid for 30 days and can be extended once for an additional 30 days. While this visa is suitable for short-term visits, it may not be ideal for digital nomads looking to stay longer. The Social-Cultural Visa, on the other hand, is designed for those who plan to stay in Indonesia for up to six months. This visa requires a local sponsor and can be extended four times, each extension valid for 30 days. The Business Visa (B211B) is another option for those conducting business activities or attending conferences, offering similar extension possibilities.

For digital nomads planning to stay longer, the Retirement Visa might be an option if you meet the age and financial requirements, although it's not designed specifically for remote workers. Another viable option is the recently introduced Digital Nomad Visa, which aims to attract remote workers to Indonesia. This visa allows digital nomads to stay for up to five years without paying local taxes, provided they earn their income from outside Indonesia.

To ensure you choose the right visa, consult with a reputable visa agent who can provide up-to-date information and assist with the application process. It's also important to stay informed about any changes in visa regulations, as policies can evolve. Properly securing your visa will allow you to focus on enjoying your stay and working productively in Bali.

Finding the Perfect Neighborhood for Long-Term Stays

Choosing the right neighborhood for your long-term stay in Bali is essential for a comfortable and productive experience. Each area of Bali offers a unique atmosphere and amenities, catering to different lifestyles and preferences. Popular neighborhoods for digital nomads include Canggu, Ubud, Seminyak, and Uluwatu.

Canggu is a favorite among digital nomads due to its vibrant community, excellent coworking spaces, and a wide variety of cafés and restaurants. The area is known for its surf culture, trendy boutiques, and lively nightlife. Canggu is ideal for those who enjoy a bustling environment with plenty of social and networking opportunities.

Ubud, on the other hand, offers a more tranquil and culturally rich experience. Surrounded by lush rice terraces and jungle, Ubud is a hub for wellness, yoga, and artistic pursuits. The slower pace of life and serene environment make it perfect for digital nomads seeking a peaceful retreat to focus on work and personal growth.

Seminyak is known for its upscale lifestyle, offering luxurious villas, high-end dining, and stylish beach clubs. It's a great choice for those who prefer a more sophisticated environment with easy access to amenities and entertainment options. Seminyak's central location also makes it convenient for exploring other parts of Bali.

Uluwatu, located on the Bukit Peninsula, is famous for its stunning cliffs, world-class surf breaks, and breathtaking sunsets. The area is less developed than Canggu or Seminyak, offering a more laid-back and scenic setting. Uluwatu is ideal for digital nomads who love outdoor activities and prefer a quieter, more natural environment.

When choosing your neighborhood, consider factors such as proximity to coworking spaces, availability of reliable internet, access to amenities, and your personal preferences for lifestyle and activities. Visiting each area and staying for a few days before making a decision can help you find the perfect fit for your long-term stay in Bali.

Accommodation Options

Bali offers a diverse range of accommodation options to suit every budget and lifestyle, making it easy for digital nomads to find a place that meets their needs. Whether you prefer a budget-friendly guesthouse, a mid-range hotel, or a luxurious villa, the island has something for everyone.

For those on a budget, guesthouses and hostels are plentiful and provide comfortable, affordable lodging with basic amenities. Areas like Ubud, Canggu, and Seminyak have a wide selection of budget accommodations that cater to digital nomads. Guesthouses often offer communal spaces, kitchens, and Wi-Fi, creating a social atmosphere where you can connect with other travelers and remote workers. Popular budget-friendly options include Puri Garden Hotel & Hostel in Ubud and The Farm Hostel in Canggu.

Mid-range accommodations, such as boutique hotels and serviced apartments, offer more comfort and amenities, including private rooms, pools, and on-site dining. These options are ideal for digital nomads looking for a balance between affordability and convenience. Places like Umah CinCin in Canggu and The Chillhouse in Seminyak provide a comfortable and productive environment with the added benefit of community activities and wellness programs.

For those seeking luxury, Bali's villa rentals offer a high-end living experience with private pools, lush gardens, and personalized services. Areas like Uluwatu, Nusa Dua, and Jimbaran are known for their upscale villas, which are perfect for digital nomads who want to work and relax in style. Villas like The Ungasan Clifftop Resort and Villa Sungai in Cepaka provide an idyllic setting with top-notch amenities and stunning views. When choosing accommodation, consider factors such as location, internet speed, and proximity to coworking spaces and amenities. Reading reviews and booking through reputable platforms can help ensure a smooth and enjoyable stay. By selecting the right accommodation, you can create a comfortable and inspiring environment that enhances your productivity and overall experience in Bali.

Integrating into the Local Community

Integrating into the local community is key to making the most of your long-term stay in Bali. Building relationships with both locals and fellow expatriates can enrich your experience and provide a support network. There are several ways to immerse yourself in the community and make meaningful connections. One of the best ways to integrate is by participating in local events and activities. Join cultural festivals, traditional ceremonies, and community gatherings to learn about Balinese customs and traditions. Ubud, in particular, offers numerous cultural events, such as dance performances, art exhibitions, and wellness retreats. Engaging in these activities not only enhances your understanding of Balinese culture but also allows you to meet new people.

Volunteering is another excellent way to connect with the local community. Organizations like Bali Children's Project, Yayasan Solemen Indonesia, and Bali Animal Welfare Association offer various volunteer opportunities. Whether it's teaching English, assisting in conservation efforts, or helping at animal shelters, volunteering enables you to give back to the community and form bonds with like-minded individuals.

Networking with other digital nomads is also essential. Bali has a vibrant digital nomad community, and joining coworking spaces like Dojo Bali in Canggu, Hubud in Ubud, or Tropical Nomad in Seminyak can facilitate connections. These spaces often host events, workshops, and social gatherings, providing opportunities to meet fellow remote workers, share experiences, and collaborate on projects.

Learning basic Indonesian phrases can go a long way in building rapport with locals. Simple greetings, expressions of gratitude, and polite inquiries show respect and willingness to engage with the local culture. Bali's friendly and hospitable people are often eager to share their customs and traditions with visitors, making integration into the community a rewarding experience.

Navigating the Local Healthcare System

Accessing quality healthcare is a crucial aspect of living in Bali, and understanding how the local healthcare system works can help you stay healthy and address any medical needs promptly.

Bali has a mix of public and private healthcare facilities, with private hospitals and clinics generally offering higher standards of care for expatriates and tourists.

Some of the reputable private hospitals in Bali include BIMC Hospital in Kuta and Nusa Dua, Siloam Hospitals in Denpasar, and Kasih Ibu Hospital in Denpasar and Kedonganan. These hospitals are well-equipped and staffed by experienced medical professionals who often speak English. They provide a wide range of services, including emergency care, specialist consultations, and diagnostic tests.

For routine medical care and minor health issues, visiting local clinics can be convenient. Clinics like Prime Plus Medical in Canggu and Ubud Health Care Clinic offer general practitioner services, vaccinations, and minor treatments. Many of these clinics also provide telemedicine services, allowing you to consult with a doctor remotely.

Pharmacies are widely available across Bali, with larger ones like Guardian and Kimia Farma offering a broad range of medications and health products. It's advisable to bring a supply of any prescription medications you regularly take, as availability may vary.

Health insurance is essential for long-term stays. Ensure your insurance plan covers international medical expenses, including emergency evacuation if necessary. Some insurance providers specialize in coverage for expatriates and digital nomads, offering comprehensive plans that include both healthcare and travel-related incidents.

Maintaining a healthy lifestyle is also important. Take advantage of Bali's wellness culture by participating in yoga classes, meditation sessions, and fitness activities. Eating a balanced diet with fresh, local produce and staying hydrated can help you stay in good health during your stay on the island.

Cultural Etiquette and Adaptation

Respecting and adapting to Balinese cultural etiquette is essential for integrating smoothly into the local community. Understanding and observing local customs not only shows respect but also enriches your experience by fostering deeper connections with the people and their traditions.

Balinese culture is deeply rooted in Hinduism, and religious practices play a significant role in daily life. When visiting temples, it's important to dress modestly, covering your shoulders and knees. Wearing a sarong and sash, which can often be rented or purchased at the temple entrance, is required. Always remove your shoes before entering temple grounds and avoid pointing your feet at shrines or statues.

Respect for elders and community leaders is a cornerstone of Balinese culture. When interacting with locals, a polite greeting with a slight bow and the word "Om Swastiastu" (a traditional Balinese greeting) is appreciated. Avoid touching people's heads, as the head is considered the most sacred part of the body. When giving or receiving something, use your right hand or both hands as a sign of respect.

Participating in local ceremonies and festivals is a wonderful way to immerse yourself in Balinese culture. Always ask for permission before taking photographs, especially during religious events. Being punctual and showing respect for the proceedings is crucial. Additionally, refrain from raising your voice or displaying anger in public, as maintaining harmony and composure is highly valued in Balinese society.

Environmental consciousness is another important aspect of cultural adaptation. Bali faces challenges with waste management and environmental conservation. As a visitor, you can contribute by reducing plastic use, participating in beach clean-ups, and supporting eco-friendly businesses. Using refillable water bottles, bringing reusable bags, and choosing sustainable products can help minimize your environmental footprint.

By embracing Balinese customs and demonstrating respect for local traditions, you will not only enhance your personal experience but also contribute to preserving the cultural integrity and natural beauty of the island.

Managing Health and Wellness

Maintaining your health and wellness is essential for a productive and enjoyable stay in Bali. The island offers numerous options for staying fit, eating well, and finding healthcare when needed.

Bali is renowned for its yoga studios and fitness centers. The Yoga Barn in Ubud is one of the most famous yoga retreat centers, offering daily classes, workshops, and wellness programs. For those in Canggu, Samadi Bali provides yoga classes and a community of wellness-focused individuals. Many coworking spaces, like Outpost, also offer on-site fitness classes and wellness programs.

Bali's food scene is rich in healthy dining options. Many cafés and restaurants cater to vegan, vegetarian, and organic diets. Places like Alchemy in Ubud and The Shady Shack in Canggu offer menus filled with nutritious and delicious plant-based dishes. Fresh tropical fruits and organic vegetables are abundant in local markets, making it easy to maintain a healthy diet.

Bali has several reputable healthcare facilities and clinics that cater to the needs of expats and digital nomads. BIMC Hospital in Kuta and Siloam Hospitals in Denpasar are among the best for general medical care and emergencies. For minor health concerns, Guardian Pharmacy and Kimia Farma provide access to a wide range of medications and health products.

To ensure your health and wellness in Bali, establish a routine that includes regular exercise, healthy eating, and sufficient rest. Stay hydrated, especially in Bali's tropical climate, and take precautions against mosquito-borne illnesses. Familiarize yourself with the location of nearby medical facilities and carry a basic first aid kit. Prioritizing your well-being will enhance your productivity and enjoyment during your stay in Bali.

Maintaining Work-Life Balance in a Tourist Paradise

Maintaining a work-life balance in Bali, where the allure of tropical beaches and cultural experiences is ever-present, requires intentional planning and discipline. As a digital nomad, it's easy to get caught up in either the work or the leisure aspects of life on the island, but achieving a balance is key to enjoying a fulfilling and productive stay.

First, establish a structured daily routine that includes dedicated work hours and leisure time. Start your day with a morning ritual that prepares you mentally and physically for work, such as yoga, meditation, or a walk on the beach. Use tools like time-blocking to manage your work tasks effectively and ensure you take regular breaks to avoid burnout.

Choose a comfortable and inspiring workspace. Bali offers numerous coworking spaces like Hubud in Ubud, Dojo Bali in Canggu, and Outpost in both Ubud and Canggu, which provide high-speed internet, ergonomic workstations, and a community of like-minded professionals. These environments not only boost productivity but also offer networking opportunities and social activities.

After work, take advantage of Bali's natural beauty and cultural offerings. Schedule time for activities that rejuvenate you, such as surfing in Uluwatu, exploring the rice terraces in Tegallalang, or attending a traditional Balinese dance performance. By balancing work with relaxation and exploration, you'll be able to maintain your productivity while fully experiencing the richness of Bali.

Tips for Long-Term Financial Planning Abroad

Long-term financial planning is essential for digital nomads living in Bali to ensure a stable and worry-free stay. Managing finances wisely helps you enjoy your time on the island without the stress of unexpected expenses or financial insecurity.

Start by creating a detailed budget that includes all potential expenses, such as accommodation, food, transportation, coworking fees, and leisure activities. Bali's cost of living can vary significantly depending on your lifestyle and location. For example, living in a luxury villa in Seminyak will cost more than staying in a budget guesthouse in Ubud.

Open a local bank account if you plan to stay for an extended period. Banks like BCA and Mandiri offer services for foreigners, making it easier to manage your money, pay bills, and avoid high international transaction fees. Additionally, using local bank accounts can provide access to better exchange rates and convenient ATM withdrawals.

Keep an emergency fund to cover unexpected expenses, such as medical emergencies, travel disruptions, or urgent repairs.

Having at least three to six months' worth of living expenses saved can provide peace of mind and financial security.

Lastly, stay informed about local tax regulations and ensure you comply with both Indonesian and home country tax laws. Consulting with a financial advisor who specializes in expatriate finances can help you navigate complex tax requirements and optimize your financial planning. By managing your finances carefully, you can enjoy a more relaxed and stable lifestyle in Bali. By following these strategies, digital nomads can achieve a harmonious work-life balance and maintain financial stability, allowing them to fully immerse themselves in the vibrant and enriching experience that Bali offers.

Internet Connectivity and Tech Support

Reliable internet connectivity is a crucial requirement for digital nomads working in Bali. While many parts of the island offer good internet services, it's essential to choose your accommodation and workspaces carefully to ensure consistent and fast internet access. Major tourist areas such as Ubud, Canggu, Seminyak, and Uluwatu have better infrastructure and more options for high-speed internet.

Most coworking spaces in Bali provide reliable high-speed internet as part of their services. For instance, Hubud in Ubud and Dojo Bali in Canggu are known for their excellent internet facilities. Additionally, many cafés and accommodations in these areas cater to digital nomads by offering robust Wi-Fi connections. However, it's always a good idea to check recent reviews and confirm the internet speed before booking.

In case of any technical issues, several tech support services are available on the island. Companies like Bali Computer

Solutions in Denpasar offer a range of services, from computer repairs to setting up home offices. They can be a valuable resource for troubleshooting and maintaining your tech setup.

For additional internet reliability, consider investing in a portable Wi-Fi device or purchasing a local SIM card with a data plan. Providers like Telkomsel and XL Axiata offer good coverage and various data packages. A portable Wi-Fi device can provide a backup internet connection, ensuring that you can stay connected even if the primary connection fails.

Legal and Financial Considerations for Long-Term Stays

Navigating the legal and financial aspects of long-term stays in Bali is crucial for a smooth and hassle-free experience. Understanding visa regulations, local laws, and financial management will help you avoid potential issues and ensure your stay is both enjoyable and compliant with Indonesian requirements. For digital nomads, choosing the right visa is the first step. As previously mentioned, the Social-Cultural Visa (B211A) and the new Digital Nomad Visa are popular choices. Each has its own requirements and duration limits, so it's important to select the one that best fits your stay length and activities.

In addition to visa considerations, understanding local laws and regulations is essential. Indonesia has strict laws regarding drug use and importation, and penalties can be severe. Be mindful of local customs and cultural norms to ensure respectful and lawful behavior. Property rental agreements should be carefully reviewed, and it's advisable to seek legal counsel if entering into long-term lease agreements. For those looking to work with local businesses or start their own, it's important to understand the requirements for work permits and business licenses.

Managing finances effectively while in Bali involves a few key considerations. Setting up a local bank account can be beneficial for handling daily expenses and transactions. Banks such as BCA, Mandiri, and BNI offer services to expatriates. Using ATMs from reputable banks to withdraw cash is generally safe, but it's wise to avoid standalone ATMs to reduce the risk of skimming. For budgeting, take advantage of the relatively low cost of living in Bali to save on expenses, but be aware of fluctuating exchange rates and transaction fees for international transfers.

For a smooth and compliant long-term stay, regularly update yourself on visa regulations and ensure your visa is valid and up-to-date. Use reputable sources and services for legal and financial matters, such as visa agents and financial advisors familiar with Indonesian laws. It's also helpful to join expatriate communities and forums where you can share experiences and get advice from others who have navigated similar challenges. By staying informed and prepared, you can focus on enjoying your time in Bali without worrying about legal and financial issues.

Coworking Spaces Across Bali

Bali has emerged as a top destination for digital nomads, offering a variety of coworking spaces equipped with modern amenities and vibrant communities. These spaces provide the perfect environment for remote work, collaboration, and networking. Whether you're based in Ubud, Canggu, or Seminyak, you'll find coworking spaces that cater to your needs.

Hubud – Ubud

Hubud is one of the most well-known coworking spaces in Bali, located in the heart of Ubud. This space offers a blend of natural beauty and modern conveniences, with fast internet, comfortable workstations, and a supportive community.

- Address: Jalan Monkey Forest 88, Ubud, Bali 80571
- Website: hubud.org

Outpost – Ubud and Canggu

Outpost has two locations in Bali, one in Ubud and another in Canggu. Both spaces offer a range of facilities, including high-speed internet, private offices, and community events. Outpost Ubud provides a serene jungle setting, while Outpost Canggu is close to the beach.

- Addresses: Ubud: Jalan Nyuh Bojog No. 13, Ubud, Bali 80571 - Canggu: Jalan Raya Semat No. 1, Canggu, Bali 80361
- Website: destinationoutpost.co

Dojo Bali – Canggu

Dojo Bali is a popular coworking space located near Echo Beach in Canggu. It offers high-speed internet, air-conditioned workspaces, and a vibrant community of remote workers. The space also hosts regular events and workshops.

- Address: Jalan Batu Mejan No. 88, Canggu, Bali 80361
- Website: dojobali.org

Tropical Nomad – Canggu

Tropical Nomad is another excellent coworking space in Canggu, known for its friendly atmosphere and excellent facilities. It offers ergonomic seating, meeting rooms, and a large garden area for breaks.

- Address: Jalan Subak Canggu, Canggu, Bali 80351
- Website: tropicalnomad-coworking.com

Biliq – Seminyak

Biliq Coworking Space in Seminyak offers a stylish and comfortable environment for remote workers. With flexible seating options, high-speed internet, and a variety of events, it's a great place to get work done and meet other nomads.

- Address: Jalan Beraban No. 36, Seminyak, Bali 80361
- Website: biliq.co

Networking and Community Events for Digital Nomads

Networking and community events are integral to the digital nomad experience in Bali, offering opportunities to connect, collaborate, and learn from other remote workers and entrepreneurs.

Bali hosts a variety of events that cater to digital nomads, ranging from professional workshops to casual meetups.

Dojo Bali Events

Dojo Bali in Canggu is known for its active event calendar, which includes workshops, skill-sharing sessions, networking events, and social gatherings. These events cover a wide range of topics, from digital marketing and entrepreneurship to wellness and personal development.

- Website: dojobali.org/events

Outpost Events

Outpost regularly hosts events at both its Ubud and Canggu locations. These events include networking mixers, business talks, yoga sessions, and creative workshops. Outpost's events are designed to foster community and support professional growth.

- Website: destinationoutpost.co/events

Ubud Writers & Readers Festival

The Ubud Writers & Readers Festival is an annual event that brings together writers, thinkers, and creatives from around the world.
It's a great opportunity for digital nomads interested in literature, storytelling, and cultural exchange.

- Website: ubudwritersfestival.com

Canggu Nomad Meetups

Canggu Nomad Meetups are informal gatherings organized by the local digital nomad community. These meetups are a great way to make new connections, share experiences, and learn about the latest trends in remote work.

- Facebook Group: Search for "Canggu Nomad Meetups"

Best Cafés for Working Remotely

Bali is home to numerous cafés that cater to digital nomads, offering not only delicious food and coffee but also a conducive environment for work.
Here are some of the best spots to consider:

Seniman Coffee Studio – Ubud

Seniman Coffee Studio is a popular café in Ubud known for its artisanal coffee and creative atmosphere. The café offers a variety of seating options, including communal tables and cozy corners, making it a great place to work. The fast Wi-Fi and delicious menu add to the appeal.

- Address: Jalan Sriwedari No. 5, Ubud, Bali 80571
- Website: senimancoffee.com

Crate Café – Canggu

Crate Café is a favorite among digital nomads in Canggu, offering a vibrant atmosphere and plenty of space to work. The café serves healthy and hearty meals, and its strong Wi-Fi makes it a reliable spot for remote work.

- Address: Jalan Canggu Padang Linjong No. 49, Canggu, Bali 80361
- Website: cratecafe.com

Coffee Cartel – Seminyak

Coffee Cartel in Seminyak is known for its Instagram-worthy interior and excellent coffee. The café provides a comfortable workspace with good Wi-Fi and a relaxed ambiance, making it ideal for remote work.

- Address: Jalan Lb. Sari No. 8, Seminyak, Bali 80361
- Website: coffeecartelbali.com

The Loft – Uluwatu

The Loft is a trendy café in Uluwatu that offers a great selection of healthy dishes and beverages. With its spacious seating, strong Wi-Fi, and laid-back vibe, it's a perfect spot for working remotely.

- Address: Jalan Labuan Sait, Pecatu, Bali 80361
- Website: theloftbali.com

Final Thoughts

Bali offers a unique blend of stunning natural beauty, vibrant culture, and modern amenities that make it an ideal destination for digital nomads. While the island is known for its picturesque beaches and lush landscapes, it also provides ample opportunities for professional growth, wellness, and community engagement. Exploring beyond the typical tourist spots can reveal hidden gems, such as tranquil villages, secluded waterfalls, and vibrant local markets, adding depth to your Bali experience.

For digital nomads, finding a balance between work and play is crucial. Taking advantage of Bali's diverse coworking spaces, engaging in local community events, and participating in cultural activities can greatly enrich your stay. The island's emphasis on wellness and sustainability also offers a chance to adopt a healthier and more mindful lifestyle, which can enhance both personal and professional well-being.

As you prepare for your stay in Bali, consider integrating into the local culture by learning a few basic Indonesian phrases and understanding local customs. Building relationships with locals and other expatriates can provide valuable support and make your time on the island more rewarding. Additionally, exploring neighboring islands such as Nusa Penida and the Gili Islands can offer fresh perspectives and new adventures.

In summary, embracing the opportunities and challenges of living and working in Bali can lead to a fulfilling and transformative experience. By staying informed, being respectful of local laws and customs, and taking full advantage of the resources available to digital nomads, you can create a productive and enjoyable lifestyle in this tropical paradise. Enjoy every moment of your journey, and let Bali inspire you in both your work and personal life.

126 BALI TRAVEL GUIDE

CHAPTER 8: MUST-HAVE CULTURAL EXPERIENCES   127

CHAPTER 8:
10 Must-Have Cultural Experiences in Bali

Experiencing the rich culture of Bali is a highlight for any visitor, offering a deep and immersive connection to the island's traditions, arts, and spiritual practices. Bali's cultural heritage is vibrant and diverse, shaped by centuries of Hindu influence, local customs, and artistic expression. Engaging in cultural activities not only enhances your understanding of Bali's unique identity but also supports the preservation of these traditions for future generations.

From participating in sacred temple ceremonies to learning traditional dance forms, Bali provides countless opportunities to explore its cultural landscape. Whether you are visiting local artisans, surfing the iconic waves, or trekking through lush rice terraces, each experience offers a glimpse into the daily life and spiritual heart of the island. These cultural activities allow you to engage with the local community, fostering a deeper appreciation for their way of life.

This chapter highlights ten must-have cultural experiences in Bali that will enrich your stay and leave you with lasting memories. By participating in these activities, you will gain insight into the island's rich heritage and create meaningful connections with its people. Let's embark on this journey to discover the essence of Bali's culture.

1. Attending a Temple Ceremony

One of the most profound ways to immerse yourself in Balinese culture is by attending a temple ceremony. These ceremonies are an integral part of Balinese Hinduism, marked by vibrant rituals, intricate offerings, and communal gatherings. Temples, or "pura," are scattered across the island, each playing a central role in the spiritual life of the community. Attending a temple ceremony offers a unique opportunity to witness and participate in these sacred practices.

The island's most significant temple ceremonies often take place during major religious festivals, such as Galungan and Kuningan, which celebrate the victory of dharma (good) over adharma (evil). Another important event is the Odalan, the anniversary of a temple's consecration, celebrated with processions, traditional music, and dance performances. Temples like Pura Besakih, Pura Ulun Danu Bratan, and Pura Tanah Lot are renowned for their grand ceremonies and stunning settings.

When attending a temple ceremony, it's important to dress respectfully and follow local customs. Wear a sarong and sash, which can often be borrowed or rented at the temple entrance. Observing silence, refraining from taking intrusive photographs, and following the lead of local participants will show your respect for their traditions. Attending a temple ceremony not only provides a deep cultural insight but also a serene and spiritual experience that connects you to the heart of Balinese Hinduism.

2. Participating in a Balinese Dance Workshop

Balinese dance is a captivating art form that combines intricate movements, expressive gestures, and elaborate costumes to tell stories from Hindu epics and local folklore. Participating in a Balinese dance workshop is an excellent way to appreciate this traditional art and engage with the island's cultural heritage. These workshops are often led by skilled dancers who guide you through the basic techniques and explain the significance behind each movement.

Balinese dance styles vary, with each dance conveying different stories and emotions. Some of the most popular forms include the Barong dance, which depicts the battle between good and evil, the Legong dance, known for its refined and intricate movements, and the Kecak dance, a mesmerizing performance involving rhythmic chanting and dramatic choreography. Learning these dances offers a unique insight into Balinese mythology and storytelling.

Many cultural centers and dance schools across Bali offer workshops for visitors. The Agung Rai Museum of Art (ARMA) in Ubud and the Bali Culture Workshop in Denpasar are among the notable places where you can take a dance class. These sessions usually begin with a brief introduction to the history and elements of Balinese dance, followed by hands-on practice. To enhance your experience, attend a traditional dance performance at venues like Ubud Palace or Pura Dalem Ubud to see the professionals in action. Participating in a dance workshop not only enriches your cultural knowledge but also provides a fun and active way to connect with Balinese traditions.

When attending a workshop, wear comfortable clothing that allows for easy movement. Be patient and open to learning, as the dance forms can be quite intricate. Taking videos or notes can help you remember the techniques and practice them later. Engaging in a Balinese dance workshop is a memorable and enriching experience that deepens your appreciation for the island's artistic heritage.

3. Visiting Local Artisans: From Batik to Silver Making

Exploring the workshops of local artisans in Bali is a fascinating way to connect with the island's rich tradition of craftsmanship. Bali is renowned for its skilled artisans who create beautiful works of art using techniques passed down through generations. Whether it's the intricate patterns of batik textiles or the delicate designs of silver jewelry, each piece tells a story of the island's cultural heritage.

In the village of Tohpati, just outside Denpasar, you can visit batik workshops where you can see the entire process of making these intricate fabrics. Batik making involves applying wax patterns to cloth and then dyeing the fabric. The wax is then removed, revealing the detailed designs. Many workshops offer hands-on experiences where you can try your hand at creating your own batik piece. Galuh Bali, one of the well-known batik centers, provides both demonstrations and classes for visitors.

Celuk Village, located near Ubud, is famous for its silver and gold jewelry. Here, you can visit numerous family-run workshops and galleries to observe the meticulous process of jewelry making. Artisans in Celuk are known for their high-quality craftsmanship, producing intricate pieces that are both beautiful and unique. Several workshops offer classes where you can learn basic silversmithing techniques and create your own piece of jewelry to take home.

When visiting these artisan workshops, take the opportunity to purchase handmade items directly from the artists. This not only supports the local economy but also provides you with a meaningful souvenir of your time in Bali. Be sure to engage with the artisans and ask about their techniques and the cultural significance of their work. This personal interaction enriches your understanding and appreciation of Bali's artistic heritage.

4. Surfing the Waves of Bali's Famous Beaches

Bali is a world-renowned destination for surfing, attracting wave enthusiasts from around the globe to its legendary beaches. The island's diverse coastline offers waves suitable for all levels, from beginners to experienced surfers. Engaging in the surfing culture of Bali not only provides an exhilarating experience but also connects you with a vital aspect of the island's modern identity. Kuta Beach is the most famous spot for beginner surfers, with its gentle waves and numerous surf schools. Here, you can take a lesson with experienced instructors who provide all the necessary equipment and guidance to get you started. Surf schools like Pro Surf School Bali and Odyssey Surf School offer lessons tailored to different skill levels, ensuring a fun and safe introduction to the sport.

For more advanced surfers, beaches like Uluwatu, Padang Padang, and Canggu offer more challenging waves. Uluwatu is known for its powerful reef breaks and stunning cliffside views, while Padang Padang hosts annual surfing competitions that attract top surfers from around the world. Canggu, with its laid-back vibe and variety of surf spots, is perfect for intermediate surfers looking to improve their skills.

When planning your surfing adventure, check the seasonal wave conditions, as Bali's surf spots can vary greatly throughout the year. The dry season (April to October) generally offers the best waves. Renting equipment is easy and widely available, but if you're serious about surfing, consider bringing your own board. Don't forget to apply reef-safe sunscreen and stay hydrated. Surfing in Bali is not just about riding waves but also about enjoying the beach culture and the stunning natural surroundings.

5. Exploring Coffee Plantations in Kintamani

Exploring the coffee plantations of Kintamani offers a delightful journey into one of Bali's most cherished agricultural traditions. The highland region of Kintamani, located at the foot of Mount Batur, provides the perfect climate and fertile volcanic soil for growing high-quality Arabica coffee. Visiting these plantations allows you to learn about the entire coffee production process, from cultivation to brewing.

Many coffee plantations in Kintamani offer guided tours that include a walk through the coffee fields, where you can see the coffee cherries growing on the trees. These tours often explain the different stages of coffee production, including harvesting, drying, and roasting. The Kintamani Coffee Plantation is one of the most popular destinations, offering comprehensive tours that end with a tasting session. Here, you can sample various types of coffee, including the famous kopi luwak, made from beans digested by civet cats.

In addition to coffee, these plantations often grow other crops such as cocoa, spices, and tropical fruits, providing a diverse agricultural experience. Visiting plantations like Bali Pulina Agro Tourism and Tegalalang Coffee Plantation not only offers insights into coffee production but also provides breathtaking views of the terraced landscapes and lush greenery of the highlands.

For a more interactive experience, consider joining a coffee-making workshop where you can roast and grind your own beans before brewing a fresh cup of coffee. These hands-on sessions provide a deeper appreciation of the effort and skill involved in producing a perfect cup. When visiting, wear comfortable walking shoes and bring a hat and sunscreen, as the tours often involve walking through the fields. Exploring the coffee plantations of Kintamani is a sensory delight that combines the beauty of Bali's landscapes with the rich flavors of its agricultural heritage.

6. Joining a Local Culinary Class

Participating in a local culinary class is an excellent way to delve deeper into Balinese culture and cuisine. These classes offer hands-on experience in preparing traditional dishes using fresh, local ingredients. From learning how to make sambal (spicy chili paste) to mastering the art of wrapping and grilling fish in banana leaves, a culinary class provides both knowledge and enjoyment.

One of the most renowned culinary schools in Bali is the Bumbu Bali Cooking School, located in Tanjung Benoa. Here, participants start the day with a guided tour of the local market to purchase fresh ingredients. The chef then leads the group through the preparation of various Balinese dishes, explaining the significance of each ingredient and cooking method. At the end of the class, participants enjoy the meal they've prepared in a communal setting.

Another popular option is Paon Bali Cooking Class in Ubud. This class takes place in a traditional Balinese home, providing an authentic setting for learning about local cuisine. Participants are involved in every step of the process, from grinding spices with a mortar and pestle to cooking over an open flame. The friendly and knowledgeable hosts ensure that the experience is both educational and enjoyable.

To get the most out of a culinary class, book in advance, especially during peak tourist seasons. Wear comfortable clothing and be prepared to spend several hours learning and cooking. Don't forget to take notes and ask for recipes so you can recreate the dishes at home. Joining a culinary class in Bali is not just about cooking; it's about immersing yourself in the island's rich culinary traditions and enjoying the flavors of Balinese culture.

7. Experiencing a Traditional Balinese Healing Session

Experiencing a traditional Balinese healing session offers a unique insight into the island's holistic approach to health and wellness. Balinese healing practices are deeply rooted in spirituality and the belief in the interconnectedness of mind, body, and spirit. These practices often combine elements of massage, herbal medicine, energy healing, and spiritual cleansing.

One of the most well-known forms of Balinese healing is the "boreh" treatment, a traditional herbal body scrub made from a mixture of spices and herbs. This treatment is believed to improve circulation, relieve muscle pain, and detoxify the body. Several wellness centers and spas across Bali, such as Karsa Spa in Ubud and Jamu Spa in Sanur, offer boreh treatments as part of their holistic healing services.

Balinese healing sessions often include consultations with a "balian" or traditional healer. These healers use a variety of techniques, including energy reading, massage, and the use of herbal remedies, to diagnose and treat ailments. The Ubud Bodyworks Center, founded by the renowned healer Ketut Arsana, offers personalized healing sessions that combine ancient techniques with modern therapeutic methods.

To fully benefit from a traditional Balinese healing session, approach the experience with an open mind and a willingness to embrace the holistic practices. Communicate any health concerns or preferences to the healer beforehand. After the session, take time to relax and reflect on the experience. Engaging in a traditional Balinese healing session can provide profound physical and spiritual benefits, offering a deeper connection to the island's culture and wellness traditions.

8. Trekking Through the Rice Terraces

Trekking through Bali's iconic rice terraces is a must-do activity that showcases the island's stunning landscapes and traditional agricultural practices. The rice terraces, with their lush green paddies and intricate irrigation systems, are not only a vital part of Bali's economy but also a symbol of its cultural heritage. Walking through these terraces offers a serene and immersive experience, connecting you with the natural beauty and rural life of the island. One of the most famous rice terrace areas is Tegallalang, located just a short drive from Ubud. The Tegallalang Rice Terraces are renowned for their breathtaking views and intricate, layered patterns. Several walking trails allow visitors to explore the terraces at their own pace, offering numerous vantage points for photography and quiet contemplation. Along the way, you'll encounter local farmers working in the fields, providing a glimpse into their daily routines.

Another excellent trekking destination is the Jatiluwih Rice Terraces, a UNESCO World Heritage site located in the Tabanan Regency. Jatiluwih offers expansive views of terraced rice fields stretching as far as the eye can see. The area features well-marked trails suitable for various fitness levels, making it accessible for most visitors. The cooler climate and less crowded paths provide a peaceful trekking experience.

For a more off-the-beaten-path experience, consider visiting the Sidemen Valley. This lesser-known area offers picturesque rice terraces and a tranquil atmosphere. Guided treks through Sidemen allow you to explore the lush countryside, visit local villages, and learn about traditional farming methods from the locals.

When planning your trek, wear comfortable walking shoes and bring plenty of water and sunscreen. Early morning or late afternoon treks are recommended to avoid the midday heat. Hiring a local guide can enhance your experience by providing insights into the agricultural practices and cultural significance of the rice terraces. Trekking through Bali's rice terraces is a memorable way to experience the island's natural beauty and connect with its rural traditions.

9. Attending a Full Moon Ceremony in Ubud

Attending a full moon ceremony in Ubud is a deeply spiritual and culturally enriching experience that offers a unique glimpse into Balinese Hindu traditions. These ceremonies, known as "Purnama," are held every month to honor the full moon, a significant event in the Balinese lunar calendar. The full moon is believed to be an auspicious time for cleansing, gratitude, and spiritual renewal, and it is celebrated with elaborate rituals, offerings, and communal gatherings.

The ceremonies typically take place in temples, with the Ubud area being a particularly vibrant location for such events. Temples like Pura Tirta Empul and Pura Gunung Kawi are renowned for their full moon celebrations. The rituals involve the presentation of intricate offerings, known as "canang sari," which are made from flowers, rice, and incense. Priests lead the ceremonies with prayers, chants, and the sprinkling of holy water, creating an atmosphere of reverence and devotion.

Visitors are welcome to attend these ceremonies, but it is important to dress respectfully and follow local customs. Wearing a sarong and sash is mandatory, and these can often be rented or purchased near the temple. It's also essential to maintain a quiet and respectful demeanor, refraining from intrusive photography and observing the rituals with mindfulness. Attending a full moon ceremony allows you to experience the spiritual heartbeat of Bali and provides a profound connection to the island's cultural and religious practices.

10. Participating in a Turtle Conservation Program

Participating in a turtle conservation program in Bali is an inspiring way to contribute to the preservation of endangered sea turtles while learning about marine conservation efforts. Bali's beaches are crucial nesting sites for several species of sea turtles, including the green turtle and the critically endangered hawksbill turtle. Conservation programs across the island work tirelessly to protect these magnificent creatures from threats such as habitat loss, poaching, and pollution.

One of the leading organizations in turtle conservation is the Bali Sea Turtle Society (BSTS) in Kuta. BSTS conducts nightly patrols during the nesting season to protect turtle nests and ensure that hatchlings reach the sea safely. Volunteers can participate in these patrols, helping to monitor nesting activity, relocate eggs to safer locations, and release hatchlings into the ocean. BSTS also conducts educational outreach to raise awareness about the importance of marine conservation.

Another significant initiative is the Turtle Conservation and Education Center (TCEC) on Serangan Island. TCEC focuses on rehabilitating injured turtles, protecting nesting sites, and educating the public about the threats facing sea turtles. Visitors can tour the facility, learn about the life cycle of sea turtles, and participate in the release of rehabilitated turtles back into the wild. This hands-on experience is both educational and deeply rewarding.

To get involved in a turtle conservation program, contact the organizations directly to inquire about volunteer opportunities and schedules. Participating in these programs not only supports vital conservation efforts but also provides a memorable and impactful experience. Remember to follow all guidelines and instructions provided by the conservation teams to ensure the safety and well-being of the turtles. By contributing to turtle conservation, you play a part in preserving Bali's natural heritage and protecting its marine ecosystems for future generations.

Final Thoughts

Engaging in these ten must-have cultural experiences in Bali offers a rich tapestry of activities that highlight the island's unique traditions, natural beauty, and community spirit. From the vibrant rituals of temple ceremonies to the serene landscapes of rice terraces and the hands-on involvement in conservation efforts, each experience provides a deeper understanding and appreciation of Balinese culture.

When planning your visit to Bali, take the time to explore beyond the popular tourist destinations. Seek out local markets, lesser-known temples, and village communities where you can interact with residents and learn about their way of life. Engaging with the local culture respectfully and authentically enhances your travel experience and supports the preservation of Bali's cultural heritage.

Additionally, consider participating in community-based tourism initiatives that benefit local residents and promote sustainable practices. These initiatives often provide more meaningful interactions and contribute to the well-being of the communities you visit. Whether it's through eco-tours, cultural workshops, or volunteer programs, your involvement can have a positive impact on both the environment and the local economy.

In conclusion, Bali's cultural richness and natural beauty offer endless opportunities for exploration and discovery. Embrace the island's traditions, respect its customs, and immerse yourself in the experiences that make Bali a truly magical destination. By doing so, you'll create lasting memories and a deeper connection to this enchanting island paradise.

BALI TRAVEL GUIDE

CHAPTER 9: RECOMMENDED ITINERARY

CHAPTER 9:
Recommended Itinerary for a 10-Day Stay

Bali is a treasure trove of experiences, offering everything from serene beaches and vibrant cultural scenes to lush jungles and towering volcanoes. Planning a comprehensive 10-day itinerary allows you to immerse yourself in the island's diverse offerings, ensuring that you experience the best Bali has to offer. This recommended itinerary is designed to help you make the most of your visit, whether you're a first-time traveler or a seasoned explorer.

Over the next 10 days, you'll journey through the bustling streets of Denpasar, delve into the artistic heart of Ubud, discover the natural wonders of Northern Bali, explore the historic sites of East Bali, and enjoy island hopping adventures to Nusa Penida and Nusa Lembongan. Each day is packed with activities that highlight Bali's unique culture, natural beauty, and welcoming spirit.

This guide will provide you with detailed plans for each day, including must-see attractions, dining recommendations, and practical tips to enhance your travel experience. Whether you're traveling solo, with friends, or family, this itinerary ensures a balanced mix of exploration, relaxation, and cultural immersion, making your trip to Bali truly unforgettable.

Planning Your Trip

Before embarking on your Bali adventure, careful planning can help you make the most of your time and avoid potential pitfalls. Start by deciding the best time to visit. Bali's dry season, from April to October, is ideal for outdoor activities, beach visits, and exploring the island's natural attractions. The wet season, from November to March, offers fewer crowds and lower prices but comes with more rainfall.

Booking your accommodation in advance is crucial, especially during peak travel seasons. Choose centrally located hotels or villas that provide easy access to the day's planned activities. For example, staying in Seminyak or Kuta for the first couple of days makes exploring Denpasar convenient, while accommodations in Ubud are perfect for experiencing the cultural heart of Bali. Northern and Eastern Bali offer quieter, more serene environments, ideal for relaxing and unwinding.

Transportation is another key aspect to consider. Renting a scooter is a popular and flexible option for getting around, but if you're not comfortable riding one, hiring a private driver or using ride-hailing apps like Grab and Gojek can be convenient alternatives. Ensure you have a good mix of activities planned, balancing sightseeing with downtime to relax and absorb the beauty around you. Finally, pack appropriately with lightweight clothing, swimwear, sunscreen, and comfortable walking shoes, as Bali's climate is warm and tropical year-round.

DAY 1: Arrival in Bali

Your Bali adventure begins with your arrival at Ngurah Rai International Airport in Denpasar. After clearing customs and collecting your luggage, head to your hotel in either Kuta or Seminyak, both conveniently located for exploring Denpasar. Take some time to settle in, freshen up, and adjust to the new surroundings.

In the evening, take a leisurely stroll along Kuta Beach, enjoying the vibrant atmosphere and beautiful sunset. Visit the Beachwalk Shopping Center for a blend of shopping, dining, and entertainment options. For dinner, head to a local warung (small restaurant) like Warung Made or Bale Udang, where you can sample traditional Balinese dishes like nasi goreng (fried rice) and sate lilit (minced fish satay).

DAY 2: Exploring Denpasar

Start your day with a visit to the Bajra Sandhi Monument, a historical monument located in the heart of Denpasar. This impressive structure commemorates the Balinese struggle against colonialism and offers insightful exhibits on the island's history. Climb to the top for panoramic views of the city.

Next, head to the Denpasar Traditional Market (Pasar Badung), Bali's largest market, where you can experience the hustle and bustle of local commerce. Explore the colorful stalls selling everything from fresh produce and spices to textiles and handicrafts. This market is a great place to pick up unique souvenirs and experience the local way of life.

Afterward, visit the Bali Museum, located nearby, which showcases an extensive collection of Balinese artifacts, including traditional costumes, ceremonial items, and historical relics. The museum's exhibits provide a deeper understanding of Bali's rich cultural heritage and artistic traditions.

In the afternoon, make your way to Sanur Beach for a more relaxed atmosphere. Sanur's calm waters and laid-back vibe make it a perfect spot for swimming and unwinding. Walk along the beachfront promenade, stopping at one of the many cafés and restaurants for a refreshing drink or a light meal. End your day with a visit to a local spa for a traditional Balinese massage, a perfect way to rejuvenate after a day of exploration.

By the end of these first two days, you will have acclimated to Bali's pace and started your journey with a blend of cultural immersion and relaxation.

DAY 3: Arrival and Initial Exploration in Ubud

Start your day by traveling to Ubud, the cultural heart of Bali, known for its lush landscapes and vibrant arts scene. Check into your accommodation, ideally located near the center of town for easy access to the main attractions. After settling in, begin your exploration with a visit to the Ubud Royal Palace (Puri Saren Agung). This historical landmark, still home to Ubud's royal family, offers a glimpse into Balinese royal life and architecture.

Next, head across the street to the Ubud Art Market (Pasar Seni Ubud), where you can browse and purchase a wide variety of handmade crafts, including textiles, jewelry, and artwork. This bustling market is an excellent place to pick up unique souvenirs and gifts.

In the afternoon, visit the Sacred Monkey Forest Sanctuary, home to hundreds of playful long-tailed macaques. Wander through the lush forest, discovering ancient temples and statues while observing the monkeys in their natural habitat. Remember to secure your belongings, as the monkeys can be quite curious.

For dinner, try one of Ubud's many renowned restaurants, such as Locavore, which offers innovative, locally-sourced cuisine, or Nusantara for a traditional Indonesian dining experience.

DAY 4: Cultural and Natural Highlights

Begin your second day in Ubud with a visit to the Tegallalang Rice Terraces, a stunning example of Bali's traditional subak irrigation system. Take a leisurely trek through the terraces, capturing the beautiful scenery and learning about the agricultural practices that sustain the local communities.

Next, head to Goa Gajah (Elephant Cave), an ancient sanctuary with intricate stone carvings, a meditation cave, and bathing pools. This site, dating back to the 9th century, provides insight into Bali's historical and spiritual heritage.

In the afternoon, indulge in a traditional Balinese cooking class at Paon Bali Cooking Class. Start with a visit to a local market to select fresh ingredients, then learn how to prepare and cook a variety of Balinese dishes under the guidance of skilled chefs. Enjoy the fruits of your labor with a delicious meal at the end of the class.

End your day with a visit to the Campuhan Ridge Walk, a scenic trail that offers breathtaking views of the surrounding hills and valleys. The gentle trek is perfect for a late afternoon stroll, providing a peaceful retreat from the busier parts of Ubud.

DAY 5: Wellness and Creativity

Dedicate your third day in Ubud to wellness and creative pursuits. Begin with a morning yoga session at The Yoga Barn, one of Ubud's most famous yoga studios. Choose from a variety of classes, ranging from gentle Hatha yoga to more vigorous Vinyasa flows, all set in a tranquil and inspiring environment.

After yoga, visit the Agung Rai Museum of Art (ARMA), which houses an extensive collection of traditional and contemporary Balinese art. The museum also offers workshops and performances, providing a deeper understanding of Bali's rich artistic traditions.

In the afternoon, explore Ubud's many boutique galleries and shops, such as Threads of Life, which showcases high-quality textiles and crafts made by local artisans. Participate in a batik or silver jewelry-making workshop to create your own piece of Balinese art.

For dinner, head to Sari Organik, a charming restaurant set in the middle of rice fields, offering organic and healthy dishes made from locally-sourced ingredients. The serene setting and fresh food make for a perfect end to your cultural exploration in Ubud.

DAY 6: Journey to Northern Bali and Lovina Beach

Depart Ubud and head towards Northern Bali, known for its tranquil beaches and lush landscapes. Your first stop is the Gitgit Waterfall, one of Bali's most picturesque waterfalls. Enjoy a refreshing swim in the natural pool and take in the surrounding beauty of the tropical forest.

Continue your journey to Lovina Beach, famous for its calm seas and black volcanic sand. Check into your accommodation and spend the afternoon relaxing on the beach or exploring the charming town of Lovina.

In the evening, dine at Spice Beach Club, which offers a range of international and Indonesian dishes in a beachfront setting. Enjoy the sunset views while savoring fresh seafood and tropical drinks.

DAY 7: Dolphin Watching and Hot Springs

Start your day early with a dolphin-watching tour off the coast of Lovina. Local boats depart at dawn to give you the best chance of seeing dolphins in their natural habitat. The experience of watching these playful creatures against the backdrop of a rising sun is truly magical.

After your dolphin adventure, head to the Banjar Hot Springs (Air Panas Banjar), located in the hills just a short drive from Lovina. These natural hot springs are set in a lush garden and feature tiered pools where you can soak and relax in the warm, therapeutic waters.

In the afternoon, visit the Brahmavihara-Arama Buddhist Monastery, Bali's largest Buddhist temple. Explore the tranquil gardens, meditation rooms, and stunning views of the surrounding countryside. This peaceful site provides a serene environment for reflection and relaxation.

For dinner, try Warung Ayu Lovina, a local favorite known for its authentic Balinese cuisine and friendly atmosphere. Enjoy traditional dishes like ayam betutu (spiced chicken) and pepes ikan (fish steamed in banana leaves) as you reflect on your northern Bali adventures.

DAY 8: Temples and Palaces of East Bali

Begin your exploration of East Bali with a visit to Besakih Temple, known as the "Mother Temple" of Bali. Located on the slopes of Mount Agung, this expansive temple complex is the most important, largest, and holiest temple of Balinese Hinduism. Wander through its various shrines and pavilions, taking in the intricate architecture and spiritual atmosphere.

Next, head to the Tirta Gangga Water Palace, a beautiful royal palace known for its lush gardens, tiered fountains, and serene water features. Spend time exploring the grounds, feeding the koi fish, and capturing photos of the picturesque surroundings.

Continue your journey to the Taman Ujung Water Palace, another stunning royal palace featuring large pools, elegant bridges, and beautifully landscaped gardens. The palace offers panoramic views of the surrounding mountains and the Lombok Strait, making it a perfect spot for leisurely exploration and photography.

In the afternoon, visit the traditional village of Tenganan, one of Bali's oldest villages. Tenganan is known for its well-preserved culture and traditions, including the unique double ikat weaving technique called geringsing. Explore the village, meet local artisans, and learn about the customs and practices that have been maintained for centuries.

For dinner, head to Warung Padang Kecag in Candidasa, a charming restaurant offering delicious Balinese and Indonesian cuisine in a tranquil garden setting. Enjoy dishes like lawar (a traditional Balinese salad) and babi guling (suckling pig) as you reflect on your day of historical exploration.

By the end of these days, you will have experienced the rich cultural heritage, natural beauty, and spiritual depth of Ubud,

Northern Bali, and East Bali, each offering a unique glimpse into the island's diverse attractions.

DAY 9: Exploring Nusa Penida

On Day 9, embark on an island-hopping adventure to Nusa Penida, one of Bali's most stunning and less-traveled destinations. Begin your day early by catching a fast boat from Sanur to Nusa Penida. The journey takes about 45 minutes, offering beautiful views of the coastline along the way.

Upon arrival, head to Kelingking Beach, one of the island's most iconic spots. The view from the cliff is breathtaking, with the beach's unique rock formation resembling a T-Rex head. If you're feeling adventurous, you can hike down to the beach, but be prepared for a steep and challenging descent.

Next, visit Angel's Billabong, a natural infinity pool formed by tide and rocks, and Broken Beach (Pasih Uug), a picturesque cove with a natural bridge. Both sites offer incredible photo opportunities and a chance to marvel at the island's rugged beauty.

In the afternoon, explore Crystal Bay, known for its clear waters and vibrant marine life. It's an excellent spot for snorkeling or simply relaxing on the beach. You can rent snorkeling gear from local vendors and spend the afternoon swimming with colorful fish and admiring the coral reefs.

For dinner, head to Penida Colada Beach Bar for a relaxing meal with a stunning sunset view. This beachfront bar offers a variety of international and Indonesian dishes, along with refreshing cocktails and a laid-back atmosphere.

DAY 10: Discovering Nusa Lembongan

On Day 10, take a short boat ride from Nusa Penida to Nusa Lembongan, another beautiful island known for its crystal-clear waters and relaxed vibe. Start your day by exploring the Yellow Bridge, which connects Nusa Lembongan to Nusa Ceningan. This vibrant yellow bridge is a popular spot for photos and a great way to get between the two islands.

Visit Dream Beach for a morning of sunbathing and swimming. The beach is renowned for its soft white sand and stunning views. Nearby, you can explore Devil's Tear, a dramatic rock formation where waves crash with incredible force, creating spectacular sprays of water.

For lunch, stop by Sandy Bay Beach Club, a chic beachfront venue offering delicious food and drinks in a relaxed setting. Enjoy fresh seafood, salads, and tropical beverages while taking in the ocean views.

In the afternoon, head to Mangrove Point for a peaceful mangrove forest tour. Rent a kayak or take a guided boat tour to explore the tranquil waters and lush greenery. The mangroves are home to various species of birds and marine life, making it a serene and educational experience.

Before heading back to Bali, spend some time at Mushroom Bay, a picturesque bay with calm waters ideal for swimming and snorkeling. The bay is lined with charming beachside cafes and restaurants where you can enjoy a final meal on the island.

Return to Bali in the late afternoon, taking the fast boat back to Sanur. Reflect on your island-hopping adventure and the incredible natural beauty of Nusa Penida and Nusa Lembongan as you make your way back to your accommodation.

Other Itinerary Options

While the 10-day itinerary covers many of Bali's highlights, there are several other options and activities you might consider if you have additional time or specific interests.
Here are a few suggestions:

Exploring the Gili Islands

Extend your island-hopping adventure by visiting the Gili Islands – Gili Trawangan, Gili Meno, and Gili Air. These islands, located off the northwest coast of Lombok, offer pristine beaches, excellent snorkeling and diving opportunities, and a relaxed island atmosphere. You can take a fast boat from Bali to the Gili Islands and spend a few days exploring each one.

Diving in Tulamben

If you're a diving enthusiast, consider a trip to Tulamben on Bali's northeast coast. The area is famous for the USAT Liberty shipwreck, one of the world's most accessible wreck dives. The dive site is teeming with marine life and offers an unforgettable underwater experience.

Cultural Immersion in Tabanan

For a deeper cultural experience, visit the Tabanan region, home to the iconic Tanah Lot Temple and Jatiluwih Rice Terraces. Tabanan offers a glimpse into traditional Balinese life, with opportunities to visit local villages, participate in cultural activities, and explore stunning natural landscapes.

Wellness Retreat in Uluwatu

Uluwatu, located on the Bukit Peninsula, is known for its dramatic cliffs, world-class surf breaks, and luxury wellness retreats. Spend a few days in Uluwatu indulging in spa treatments, yoga sessions, and healthy cuisine while enjoying the breathtaking ocean views.

Adventure Activities in Bali

For thrill-seekers, Bali offers a range of adventure activities, including white-water rafting on the Ayung River, paragliding over the cliffs of Uluwatu, and ATV tours through rice paddies and jungle trails. These activities provide an adrenaline rush and a unique way to explore Bali's diverse landscapes.

Final Thoughts

Bali is a destination that captivates the heart and soul of every traveler with its unique blend of natural beauty, rich culture, and warm hospitality. Whether you're exploring the vibrant streets of Denpasar, delving into the artistic heart of Ubud, marveling at the natural wonders of Northern and Eastern Bali, or island hopping to Nusa Penida and Lembongan, each experience adds a new layer to your understanding and appreciation of this magical island.

For digital nomads, Bali offers a welcoming environment with modern amenities, vibrant coworking spaces, and a supportive community. Take advantage of the opportunities to connect with other remote workers, immerse yourself in local culture, and maintain a healthy work-life balance.

As you plan your trip, remember to approach your travels with an open mind and a spirit of adventure. Bali's beauty lies not just in its famous landmarks but also in its hidden gems and the genuine connections you make along the way. Respect the local customs, support sustainable tourism practices, and take time to enjoy the simple pleasures of island life.

In the wise words of J.R.R. Tolkien, "Not all those who wander are lost." Embrace the journey, explore the wonders of Bali, and create memories that will last a lifetime. Selamat jalan (safe travels) and enjoy every moment of your Balinese adventure!

Conclusion

Bali, a gem of the Indonesian archipelago, captivates visitors with its diverse landscapes, vibrant culture, and serene spirituality. Throughout this guide, we've delved into the island's many facets, from its bustling urban centers to its tranquil rural retreats, offering you a comprehensive roadmap for an unforgettable stay. Each chapter has illuminated a different aspect of Bali, inviting you to engage deeply with its beauty and charm.

Exploring Bali means immersing yourself in a place where the sacred and the everyday coexist harmoniously. Whether you're marveling at the intricate carvings of ancient temples, witnessing a traditional dance performance, or simply soaking in a sunrise over the rice paddies, Bali offers a continuous feast for the senses. This island is not just a destination; it's a journey into a lifestyle that embraces balance, mindfulness, and a profound connection to nature.

The true essence of Bali lies in its people. The Balinese are renowned for their warmth, hospitality, and strong sense of community. Engaging with locals, whether through participating in a religious ceremony, learning about traditional crafts, or sharing a meal, provides insights into their way of life that go beyond the typical tourist experience. This cultural immersion enriches your visit and leaves you with a deeper appreciation of the island's heritage and values.

For digital nomads, Bali is a haven of productivity and inspiration. The island's growing network of coworking spaces, coupled with its scenic beauty and vibrant expatriate community, creates an ideal environment for remote work. Whether you're setting up your laptop in a bustling café in Canggu or a serene coworking space in Ubud, the balance of work and leisure is easily achieved in Bali.

Respecting local customs and the environment is paramount to preserving Bali's charm. Embrace sustainable travel practices by choosing eco-friendly accommodations, supporting local businesses, and minimizing your environmental footprint. Engage in activities that promote conservation and cultural preservation, such as beach clean-ups or workshops on traditional crafts. By doing so, you contribute positively to the island's future while enriching your own experience.

To make your journey smoother and more engaging, here are some useful Indonesian phrases:

- "Halo" – Hello
- "Terima kasih" – Thank you
- "Tolong" – Please
- "Berapa harganya?" – How much does it cost?
- "Di mana kamar mandi?" – Where is the bathroom?
- "Nama saya..." – My name is...
- "Bisakah Anda membantu saya?" – Can you help me?
- "Kopi, tolong" – Coffee, please
- "Selamat pagi" – Good morning

- "Selamat malam" – Good night
- "Saya tidak bisa bicara bahasa Indonesia dengan baik" – I don't speak much Indonesian
- "Di mana...?" – Where is...?
- "Saya ingin..." – I would like...
- "Saya tersesat" – I'm lost

Your time in Bali will be filled with moments of wonder and discovery. Whether you're exploring the bustling markets of Denpasar, relaxing on the beaches of Nusa Penida, trekking through the lush jungles of Ubud, or diving into the vibrant underwater world, each experience adds a unique thread to the tapestry of your journey.

Embrace Bali's spirit of harmony and openness. Allow yourself to be moved by its natural beauty, inspired by its cultural depth, and connected by its sense of community. Travel not just to see new places, but to grow, learn, and become part of the world in a more profound way.

As you reflect on your travels, remember that the true beauty of Bali lies not just in its landscapes, but in the moments of connection and understanding that you experience along the way. Here's to the adventures that await you, the friendships you'll forge, and the memories you'll cherish long after you leave the island's shores.

Selamat jalan (safe travels) and enjoy every moment of your Balinese adventure. Bali is more than a destination; it's a journey of the heart and soul, a place where you can find peace, inspiration, and a deeper connection to the world around you.

CONCLUSION

Made in the USA
Las Vegas, NV
31 January 2025